D0746114

THE UNPREPARED SOCIETY

This Colophon paperback edition reprints Number Ten of the John Dewey Society Lecture Series, originally published by Basic Books, Inc.

THE UNPREPARED SOCIETY: Planning for a Precarious Future

BY

Donald N. Michael

FOREWORD BY

Ward Madden

CHAIRMAN, COMMISSION ON LECTURES, THE JOHN DEWEY
SOCIETY FOR THE STUDY OF EDUCATION AND CULTURE

HARPER COLOPHON BOOKS
Harper & Row, Publishers
New York, Evanston and London

First HARPER COLOPHON edition published 1970 by
Harper & Row, Publishers, Inc.

FOREWORD

BY WARD MADDEN

Chairman, Commission on Lectures
The John Dewey Society for the Study of Education and Culture

THE LAST FEW YEARS have seen the rise of an activity that Donald N. Michael calls "futurism." It is one of the striking phenomena of the times, and takes many forms, *The Unprepared Society* itself being one example. Futurists are men who are using rather recently developed intellectual and scientific techniques, as well as some older methods, to anticipate social and technological developments years or decades before they occur. Most of them are also concerned with the problems of preparing to cope with the conditions they forecast, and most of them are aware of, or are involved in, the realities of the effort to organize society politically to confront its futures. Hence Andrew Kopkind has called them "the future-planners," while Bertram Gross has dubbed them "technopols."

Although current examples of futurism vary in quality, viability, and direction, their proliferation suggests a trend.

Buckminster Fuller's World Resources Inventory, Bertrand de Jouvenel's Futuribles, Mankind 2000, and the Delphi Technique (associated with the Rand Corporation) for forecasting a range of social and technological developments are only a few among numerous efforts. While financial support for such enterprises is often faltering, the variety of sponsors—governmental, industrial, academic, and private—suggests that something is indeed going on.

This interest in future-planning is particularly noteworthy in view of the fact that since World War II serious concern with social-economic planning has lain relatively dormant. As Donald N. Michael notes, a scientifically grounded movement toward social-economic planning made a beginning in this country under the stimulus of the New Deal. Calls for the reconstruction of the social order were heard in many quarters. Despite the sometimes bitter differences between them, neo-Marxian ideologues and Deweyan social democrats were often able to join forces to support progressive social reforms. The emphasis on general planning in society overflowed into educational thinking and practice, and affected them profoundly. Shortly before the election of Roosevelt, George Counts stirred many an educator with his challenge: *Dare the Schools Build a New Social Order?*

Although far from being the first historical example of a call upon the schools to spearhead social reform, Counts' book, along with the milder William H. Kilpatrick's *Education and the Social Crisis,* heralded an era spanning the 1930's and 1940's, when a number of educators, particularly those associated with the social reconstructionist wing of the progressive education movement, saw the school as an instrument in bringing about a society characterized by contin-

uous social-economic planning. Those were the days of the
Social Frontier, which declared in bold type on the cover of
its first issue that *laissez faire* was dying and that a collectivist age was emerging. For more than nine years its contrib-
utors, including such educationists as Kilpatrick, Counts,
Boyd Bode, and John Childs, as well as other intellectuals
such as Charles Beard, Lewis Mumford, and John Dewey,
wrote on various aspects of the school's role in promoting the
new age of social planning and control.

Meanwhile, the famed social studies textbooks of another
Social Frontier contributor, Harold Rugg, became so popular
all through the schools, from the primary grades through
high school, that the schools seemed, to conservatives, to be
well on their way to doing just what Counts and others were
asking them to do. These books emphasized social problems
and, in Rugg's phrase, "frontier thinking." Finally, in the
1940's the American Legion led a campaign that drove these
books out. Other interests and attitudes began to dominate
America, which now entered a paradoxical period of the illu-
sion of fully shared affluence, and the reality of political and
social alienation. Social-reconstructionism both in the social
scene generally and in the schools seemed dead, with such
exceptions as Theodore Brameld's efforts in the late 1940's
and in the 1950's to promote a "future-centered education."

Many an older school man, looking at the table of con-
tents of *The Unprepared Society,* will feel a nostalgic thrill
and a stirring in the old bones when he sees some of the
chapter titles, particularly the one on long-range planning.
He will be disappointed. Today's futurists, and particularly
Donald N. Michael, are a new breed, bearing little resem-
blance to the social planners of the 1930's. Their ideas are

both more sophisticated and less satisfying to ideologues than those of their predecessors.

It is interesting to ask, then, two questions: Why has futurism re-emerged in a new form? And in what ways is the new futurism different from the old?

Writing in *The Public Interest,* Daniel Bell listed several factors to help account for the new interest in the future. These include a renewed optimism, stimulated by remarkable technological developments and the prestige of science, about possibilities of meeting basic human needs and of defining new, worthwhile, and realizable goals; greater interdependence in society created by new developments in transportation and communication; a national commitment to economic growth; and the development of a new intellectual technology—cybernetics, information theory, and so on—making long-range social and technological forecasting a more feasible undertaking than before. If we discount the eudaemonism of the above account (such cheerfulness hardly seems warranted in a society in which signs of restlessness, cynicism, revolt, and wanting to drop out are pervasive), there may be much validity in it.

Perhaps the greatest impulse to trying to foresee and plan the future comes from the combination of having new tools with which to do it and the growing realization that every technological and social innovation has repercussions which spread like a wave through the complex interlinked sections of society. What has virtually forced the new futurism into existence is the extraordinary bigness, the piles of money at stake, and the complexity of intersecting interests involved in almost any significant corporation or government operation or project. There is as much desperation as optimism here.

Aside from this, it seems likely that concern with the future is so characteristic of being human that any loss of futuristic interest, such as that in the 1950's, is bound to be temporary. Man lives in a more extended time dimension than do other animals; he reacts not merely to the immediate present, but to a present extended into past and future by his ability to foresee and plan results in the light of experience. In Korzybski's phrase, man is a time-binder. No other animal had the intellectual potential to have the slightest interest in reading tea leaves, or in developing future-centered theories of personal or social salvation as religion and Marxism have done.

If we compare earlier efforts at scientific forecasting and planning, such as those of the New Deal era, with the new futurism, the differences are several. For one thing, the new effort approaches its tasks in a deliberately more piecemeal way, seeking to define an appropriately extended but practically delimited context for each problem. No effort is made to relate forecasting to a grand theory, or to a theory of history (Marx's predictions about the course of capitalistic society are the classic example). And no effort is made to relate planning to Mannheimian ideological or utopian rationales, as planning during the New Deal era tended to do.

The new futurists are more cautious in certain ways than were their predecessors. One of their marks is their tendency to talk about a multitude of possible futures and to avoid talk of *the* future. *If* certain things are done or not done, future "x" rather than future "y" will be more likely to result. But the conditions that might lead to "y" must be studied too, if we are to understand the choices and possibilities before us. Furthermore, a deliberate effort is made to make prophecies self-fulfilling. They are elaborated with a detail that makes possible performing the acts that will help bring them about—this, in fact, is virtually a definition of what planning is.

The new futurism, like the old, is concerned with the economic and technological aspects of the future. But more than did the old, it integrates these concerns with the psychological and sociological dimensions of the future, with the human emotional and attitudinal conditions, responses, objectives, and with the belief-systems, culture processes, subcultural interactions that must be taken into account.

But perhaps most of all the new futurism is distinctive in the novelty and power of the intellectual and other tools that are available to it. Systems analysis, elaborate simulation techniques, automated access to central data banks, information theory, game theory, and the use of socio-economic models, often mathematically stated, all aided and abetted by the computer, make possible a massive application of data not hitherto possible.

The reader of *The Unprepared Society* will find all of the above characteristics displayed there or commented upon in greater or less degree. But even though Donald N. Michael may share these tendencies with his fellow futurists, he is notably different from the majority of them in two ways. For one thing, being a social psychologist, he pays even more attention to the psychological and to the cultural-process ramifications of our society's possible futures than do most of his peers.

But even more striking is his not sharing with them their general millenarian tendency. The new futurists, with some exceptions, share one characteristic with their earlier prede-

cessors. They tend to be optimists. No one today any longer
believes in the inevitability of progress, but many of today's
futurists have become bedazzled by the real opportunities for
progress that are opening up. For example, Emmanuel Mesthene of Harvard, executive director of the IBM-sponsored
program on Technology and Society, believes that man has re-
gained his nerve and is ready to move ahead. Such futurists
are not in tune with the Augustinian-Freudian view of uncon-
trollable, self-destroying impulses in man that make him
capable of throwing away his own best chances. True
enough, futurists have called attention to grim and dangerous
possibilities—pesticides, pollution, drugs, overpopulation,
overloading of cities, loss of privacy, loss of control due to
complexity, and the rest. But the tendency, except for a few
skeptics here and there, is to regard such problems as essentially soluble. No doubt they are, if man's unqualified use of
his rationality is assumed. That assumption, perhaps, links
old and new futurists, from at least the time of Marx, in a
common brotherhood. Crediting man with more rationality
than he possesses is perhaps an occupational hazard for futurists of all generations, for planning itself is an effort to ex-
orcise irrationality.

Not that Donald N. Michael writes in the voice-of-doom
tradition of elitist critics of mass society. Nor does he believe
either in original sin or the death instinct. There are, he says,
no villains and heroes in his story. But he is poignantly aware
of the irrationalities built into the structure of the already
emerging society of the future, with its "complexity, turmoil,
and scarcity." Among the worst scarcities are time and tal-
ent. But there is no scarcity of institutionalized resistance to
change. As we become a future-planning society on a mas-

sive scale, an insurmountable intellectual gap may develop between the planners and those being planned for. The ethical basis for a decent society may be more difficult to maintain. Thus the future-planning society has built into its own structure a schiztic and continuing struggle between rationality and irrationality. The outcome is not preordained, nor probably ever finally settled.

Since educational institutions are subject to the same difficulties that beset the new society generally, Michael does not turn to them as the panacea. Hence his educational proposals may seem too modest to the old-time school man hoping for another bugle call of the *Dare the Schools Build a New Social Order?* tone. Michael is too aware of the scarcities in existing educational resources—as much intellectual and emotional as material—to make any such sweeping call to arms. Instead, in the more modest but effective problem-by-problem mode of the new professional futurist, he raises questions and dilemmas for the school man. We do not yet know enough to solve them, but all the more do they need pondering. In the Deweyan phrase, to ask the right questions is to point the way toward the right answers.

June 1968

ACKNOWLEDGMENTS

Ward Madden combined his critique of the first draft of this book with those of Arno Bellack and Richard McAdoo into sensitive and incisive observations and questions that were especially valuable for clarifying and focusing the final manuscript. I am indebted to these three and especially to Ward Madden, whose counsel has gone well beyond this. Henri and Rita Wiegers have my appreciation for conscientiously and imaginatively playing "typical reader," thereby helping me to remove obscurities and awkwardnesses.

My wife's contributions are unique. Through her involvement in volunteer teaching of disadvantaged youngsters, she has revealed much to me about the professional/nonprofessional issue and about the pedagogical difficulties facing educators who are sensitive to the demands the future imposes. And her good-natured coping with the tensions and tempers of book writing allowed me to keep in touch with my family. Without this kind of emotional nourishment and daily experience, books such as this tend to become separated from the very ways of being they are supposed to be concerned about.

DONALD N. MICHAEL

August 1968

CONTENTS

CONTENTS

THE UNPREPARED SOCIETY

🌿 1 🌿

ON THE ENVIRONMENT
OF THE FUTURIST [1]

THE GENERAL ARGUMENT of this book is that the convergence of certain social and technological trends will lead to much more extensive use of long-range planning even though we are ill prepared institutionally, methodologically, and personally to do it well; and that the type of education needed to realize the opportunities and avoid the threats in this situation is not at all likely to be available as soon as we will need it or on the required scale.

In what follows, we will be examining trends and circumstances *during* the next couple of decades or so. The last few years have seen the efflorescence of all sorts of preoccupations with the future and with our capabilities for planning for it and "inventing it," to use Dennis Gabor's influential

[1] The term "futurist" categorizes those people who are seriously concerned with explicating the characteristics of future trends and circumstances and with developing the methods for detecting and evaluating the import of these characteristics.

3

metaphor. This new attention in intellectual circles, and in political ones too, has generated a vast variety of arguments, dialogues, "invisible colleges," [2] conferences, commissions, work groups, publications, and other devices intended to enlarge understanding and produce a climate for action or at least for awareness. As a result, thinking about what the future alternatives and likelihoods may be, and what their implications are, has become a far more involved area of serious study than it used to be. There are so many ideas being hawked in the marketplace that what one is exposed to is partially a matter of who yells loudest or whom one happens to be standing nearest to. What one hears needs to be assessed for reliability and insight, and because of the relatively footless nature of the topic, one must be especially critical of one's own views as well as the other fellow's. There are polemical jungles that must be hacked through to see if they hide rare new thoughts. Also, one must evaluate the "authoritative statements" of scientists, engineers, industrialists, and government spokesmen who seek the image of "social awareness" and the "big view," as they describe the future in terms of gee-whiz technology and conventional wisdom about man and his nature. In this new and amorphous area, one must keep especially close track of what others are thinking—or at least are publicly saying—in order to be able to decide what needs thinking about.

I begin with this recital of modish intellectual and entre-

[2] "Invisible college" is Derick de Sola Price's term to refer to the continuing activities of informal small groups whose members hone the cutting edge of new knowledge. These people do not depend on the ponderous procedures of publications and formal meetings to exchange ideas and information but use instead the telephone, the mimeograph, and their own especially organized work groups.

preneurial hecticness because it is background for appreciating the significance of certain factors that affect social forecasting today, and that will continue to affect it in the years ahead. These include the methodological difficulties and personal motivations that inevitably enter into serious efforts to forecast tomorrow's possibilities. Both play critical roles in the arguments and counterarguments that develop around the increasingly important activity of making forecasts depicting futures—an activity, as I shall argue later, that will increasingly be a central requirement for operating tomorrow's world.

Some who speculate about the future do so for the intellectual and aesthetic rewards such an exercise provides. But many who do the speculating, and essentially all of those who seriously respond to it, do so because they hope to influence the future through acts taken in the present. And even when the author of a speculation is more modest or diffident in his intentions, his supporters and critics will respond to his work as if it were intended to or able to influence present actions. Thus, a preoccupation with the future usually has a political state of mind associated with it: the desire to influence present actions and the beliefs upon which they are based in order to make preferred futures more likely—whether the object of influence is a particular child or a national organization.

What's more, since what happens over the years ahead in large degree will be outgrowths of present societal characteristics, forecasts about the next five to twenty-five years or so necessarily are based on implicit or explicit interpretations of what is happening now and why it is happening. Hence, those who see themselves as participating in making the future—

and I most definitely include here my fellow "futurists"—either feel threatened (and angered) or supported (and pleased) by the implied repudiation or acceptance books of this sort supply for what they believe about the present and how it got this way, and what they want to believe about the future and how it will get its way. If the forecasts do not fit their views of what is right and wrong about society today and tomorrow, they will find fault, partially in order to convince their most salient audiences (and themselves) that their explanations and preferences are still valid, still right. The obverse holds, too, of course. Thus, a prediction about the future can be interpreted as a repudiation or legitimation of both the explanation and the delineation of what is and what could be. As a result, there are very few neutral producers, critics, or users of social forecasts.

These usually unexpressed or unexamined political, emotional, and ideological interests in both the writer and reader —and they are there even when the analyst insists his work is "value-free"—encourage the reader to overlook, misunderstand, or misinterpret. Some forearming of the reader may be accomplished if I warn him of the typical ways he or others may misread and misinterpret what follows here, or in the writings of other futurists, for that matter. For much of what I will be drawing attention to is threatening to senses of self, status, and purpose, and there are typical ways to defend oneself against such threats. (Again, I emphasize, based on personal bruises, I am including among "readers," writers' readings of other writers.) These consist of not remembering the author's choice of points of emphasis and the qualifying context he provides for them; of translating and transforming what the author emphasizes into a syntax with which the reader is comfortable and familiar, thereby shifting the plane of discourse; of judging the validity of the author's argument by his mood—optimistic or pessimistic—rather than by its content. There is one other easy out for those too threatened: the smug opinion that if one is going to criticize, one has the obligation to provide answers for the question one poses. When this quid pro quo is the criterion for serious attention, it saves the reader the embarrassment and anxiety of having to face up to questions for which there are no good available answers. We know from much psychological research that threatening information will be ignored if it is threatening enough and if no means for reducing the threat are provided along with the information. But some people are able to face more intense emotional threats than others, and it is for these people that I write. For I have few if any answers, and these in turn raise more questions than they answer. Some authors are more supportive, more sanguine in future viewpoint; some are more threatening. In part, they are so because of what they believe about the future, in part, out of what they assess as the degree of threat or optimism most likely to get attention for what they believe.

At any rate, the convergence of such defenses, of differing motives, of varying perspectives, produces an atmosphere of conflicting and contending, polemics, reports, analyses, and books, each seeking its audience, each trying to capture an audience, especially a powerful one. Each couches its findings in the rhetoric of facts, authorities, careful methodology, historical precedent, etc. But the only fact that really holds up is that forecasting the directions of alternate futures on the basis of what is happening and has happened necessarily depends on far too few reliable and valid facts. Most of what passes for "the truth" on these matters is better typified by the image of the expert with both feet planted firmly in midair. In general, we don't have enough data about society to know what, in detail, is happening to us, much less what will happen to us, especially as a function of technological change. An example is useful here.

This data-poor condition is true even with regard to the much argued-about topic of the present and future impact of cybernation on the work force. In spite of many books and reports arguing the matter to one decimal place, there are today no adequate sources of economic and work-force data for decisively answering the questions with the subtlety required: too often assumptions substitute for facts. Consider the words of the economist Herbert E. Striner, Director of Program Development for the W. E. Upjohn Institute of Employment Research, with regard to the much heralded 1966 report of the National Commission on Technology, Automation, and Economic Progress. The Commission was supposed to provide answers to questions having to do with "new job requirements and the major types of worker displacement . . . likely to occur during the next 10 years." After analyzing the report and its six volumes of background studies, Striner concludes:

The Commission chooses to answer by accepting a series of assumptions which obliterate the very problem under investigation. Unemployment is assumed to be 3 percent; no major changes in technology are envisioned as being possible in terms of anything less than roughly 14 years; and the categories of occupation are so broad as to defy any meaningful discussion regarding skills or job descriptions.[3]

[3] Herbert E. Striner, "Technological Displacement as a Micro Phenomenon," *Monthly Labor Review*, XC, No. 3 (March 1967), 30–31.

The data situation is even less clear when it comes to documenting the specific impacts of technology on poverty, or on the conditions for affective learning, or on the use and amount of leisure time, or on the effects of urban crowding, and so on through the whole set of social consequences that we *believe*—but do not know for sure—have the characteristics they do partly as a result of technological developments. The enormous conceptual and operational tasks involved in deciding what data would provide the basis for valid and reliable interpretations of what is happening to our society are brilliantly set out in *Social Indicators*.[4] This book makes amply clear that, for the most part, we literally don't know what we are talking about when we attempt to quantify complex cause-and-effect relationships among societal processes.

When it comes to forecasting the future, our "facts," which must be based on methods that use extrapolation, precedent, appeal to authority (i.e., expertise), or imagination, are in much worse shape. For we have no proven means for predicting the future whether they are the arcane methods of systems analysis or operations research, with or without computer assist, or the age-old one of consulting the expert, the seer, whatever his modern trappings.[5] What methods we have been trying out have not been validated because it is only in the last few years that we have begun to be seriously concerned about making long-range forecasts about complex aspects of societal change, and the futures which we have

[4] Raymond A. Bauer (ed.), *Social Indicators* (Cambridge, Mass.: M.I.T. Press, 1966).

[5] In view of this state of affairs, I especially want to emphasize that when I use "will" to refer to future possibility it is only meant to suggest what seems to be a particularly good bet. I will use "will" sometimes simply to break the tedium of "very likely," "very probably," "highly likely," and so on. I make no claims to precognition.

struggled to foresee have not happened yet. As of now, we are not even good at predicting that socially crucial factor: long-range birth rates. And recent studies by the National Bureau of Economic Research show that beyond six months the accuracy of short-range business forecasts diminishes so rapidly as to make them of little or no value.[6] Partly the difficulty of forecasting results from inadequate or nonexistent data about those aspects of society that one needs to measure in order to predict. More fundamentally, it is a matter of inadequate or nonexistent theory about the nature of complex social processes: we know relatively little about *what* to measure or observe in order to predict well.

As later chapters will try to show, this situation is almost certain to improve as a result of a growing attention to the long-range planning of human support services and as a result of powerful computer-based techniques for manipulating vast amounts of data in complex ways. But even with these improvements there will still be the exceedingly difficult theoretical task of dealing with discontinuities which inevitably arise in the evolution of societies. Among other causes, these discontinuities will result from unanticipated consequences from the application of powerful technologies. Also, as we seem to be experiencing more frequently, they very likely will result from protest-type and insurrectionist political actions deliberately undertaken to disrupt the status quo. Theories in general are unable to deal with discontinuities, though eventually social theory may be better able to indicate possible sources or precursors of crises so that, for better or worse, they can be avoided through planning.

If these caveats are valid, what is the point of making

6 Victor Zarnowitz, "On the Accuracy and Properties of Short-Term Economic Forecasts," *Annual Report,* National Bureau of Economic Research, June 1965, pp. 16–25.

forecasts or of paying attention to them? There are three reasons for doing so, all of them deriving from the fact of life that present acts will more or less determine the future, in many cases the more so if we choose to act with that intent—and in many cases we will have to so choose, as we shall see. In the first place, some of the forecasts are likely to be close to the mark; if we attend to them, we at least reduce the chances of being taken unawares by the future. In the second place, if we take some forecasts seriously, they provide a better basis than no forecasts for generating the conditions for self-fulfilling prophecies. That is, defining reality thus and so often leads to acting in ways that in fact make it so. In the third place, well-done forecasts help us pay more attention to the many factors that interact to produce the present and, from it, the future. As such, long-range forecasts should help us become more sophisticated about which factors in the situation may determine what alternatives there may be, and about the consequences of pursuing some alternatives rather than others. Thus, we can plan better.

All in all, I believe what I argue here does reflect a significant developing reality: as of now I could not argue an opposite "reality" with any personal conviction. While I believe what I am saying, at the same time I recognize that I am subject to the motives and methods of those concerned with alerting others to the directions of the future. Some others more or less share my view of "reality," and these I will quote or refer to to enhance my arguments. I am not giving a "balanced" picture, if this means presenting "all sides." [7] I wouldn't know how to recognize such, given the state of fore-

---

[7] Even within my biases certain aspects of the present and speculated-on future have been stressed at the sacrifice of others. Indeed, some issues are herein raised more than once for the ad-

casting and forecasters that I've described. Moreover, even consensus on particular forecasts would be unconvincing to me. Such consensus would necessarily be based on too simplified an approach to the issues, given the methodological inadequacies described earlier. But just as important as consensus, the directions and circumstances that characterize the future will depend in many cases on precisely the fact that there *is* dissensus among experts about values, applications, consequences, personalities, and all the other things that produce the dialectic of change. As we shall see, one of the critical challenges we face is to develop social institutions for increasing the means for distributing, examining, comparing, integrating, and acting on *different* forecasts.

Meantime, the reader will have to depend on himself to seek out alternative viewpoints; and in this day of the "invisible college," where the most recent thinking is exchanged among those working on a topic by voice or mimeograph, he'll have to depend on luck or insiders to expose him to the alternatives. A word of caution, however: in the heated atmosphere in which flourish the "futurists" and those ana-

---

ditional significance they gain when examined in different contexts. (In my previous book, *The Next Generation: Prospects Ahead for the Youth of Today and Tomorrow* [New York: Random House, 1965], many aspects of tomorrow's world are explored that are underemphasized or unmentioned here.) Since I am trying to develop an argument rather than to present a finished position, this approach is warranted here. What follows then are several essays-in-process. They are not, I hope, merely jumbled together, but neither do I expect them to present an arresting finished conceptual edifice. In particular, there are other "last chapters" to be written in addition to the one here, chapters on needed changes in political processes, in the relationship of private interests, as pursued in large corporations, to the public interest, etc. However, since this book is an extension of my address to The John Dewey Society, it is limited to a final chapter on some aspects of education.

lyzing the present for what it might say about the future, there is less than conventional adherence to customary standards of identifying the opposition or the sources of some of one's ideas. The reader will not always know whose ox is being gored, or who is not being footnoted or invited to this or that important conference. Sometimes this is a matter of polemics, sometimes politics, sometimes personalities, scrabbling for attention or trying to keep others from being attended to, and sometimes it's a matter of being too lazy or having too little time to carefully take apart another's arguments in order to make one's own. I am not immune to demonstrating some of these unscholarly, even ungentlemanly inadequacies and I know others have practiced theirs on me.

With these observations in mind about the motives and methods of making and responding to forecasts about the future of society, we can go on to other matters. I will, however, further examine these factors from time to time, because in one form or another they will be significantly involved in the ways we go about preparing for the future and interpreting "it" when "it" arrives—in order to prepare for the further future.

2

ONE WAY OF LOOKING AT TOMORROW: COMPLEXITY, TURMOIL, AND SCARCITY

Complexity

We expect in the United States, by about 1975, about 220 million people; by 1980, 235 million people. By 1975, about 50 percent of the population will be under 25, and the percent over 65 will have increased by at least 20 percent over what it is today, to more than 22 million. Probably they will increase more than this as chemotherapy, electromechanical implants, computer-assisted hospital care, and better management (for example, Medicare) improve and sustain the health of older people so that more of them live longer.

Part of our complexity will be the result of world population size—4 billion by about 1977—and in particular the number of people in what we have optimistically been calling the emerging nations. Two figures symbolize something of the coming confrontation that world represents for us. As of

14

now, 50 percent of the population in the emerging world is under 15 years old. By 1975, the population in the emerging world under 15 years old will equal the total population of the developed world. Thus, even with successful birth control in these areas (and the chances are we won't have widespread successes with birth control over the short run) we face an enormous surge in the size of the dependent populations of those countries; and, with it, a set of problems of enormous scope and scale. However, there may not be such population growth; famine and epidemics very likely will kill hundreds of millions. Then we will face additional ethical as well as operational complexities. Probably we will be faced with a combination of famine, epidemics, and too large populations.[1]

This unprecedented world population will be living in expanding urban areas. In the United States, about 80 percent of our population will be living in urban areas by about 1980. As old cities fuse and as new cities are deliberately constructed in the spaces between them, these urban areas will be changing from the traditional pattern of geographically separated cities, each with its distinct political and physical characteristics and social identification, into megalopolises—regional urban areas. (The process is very nicely

[1] Except for occasional comments such as this, I have not explored here the possible implications of international developments for the directions of our society. What happens beyond our borders very well may affect what happens here as much as anything domestic does—as the Vietnam tragedy demonstrates. Also, other countries are experimenting with planning under various political philosophies and these will provide us with important leads for our own experiments. But in a small book there is just so much that can be attended to. This caveat is a token of international awareness on my part and an alerting signal to the reader to keep his own knowledge of world trends in mind as he reads this.

demonstrated by the simultaneous fusing of Baltimore and Washington, while the new city for 120,000, Columbia, Maryland, is also being built between them. And Columbia, which will be extraordinarily attractive, will draw more people yet to the region.) The East Coast megalopolis is already apparent, stretching from about Bangor, Maine, to Norfolk, Virginia. The Middle West megalopolis will spread from Chicago, over to Detroit and Cleveland, and down to St. Louis. Another megalopolis is in formation along the eastern coast of Florida. The same development is under way all over the world.

By the turn of the century, if present trends continue unchecked, San Francisco will have become part of a super megalopolis stretching . . . to the Mexican border, 500 miles to the south, and containing 40 million people. This strip city will house 174 million Americans on urbanized land ranging in density from 660 to 2,600 people per square mile.[2]

A third contribution to complexity will derive from an expanding demand for human support services, welfare services not only for the poor but for everyone. We are familiar with recent evidences of these demands as expressed in the tardy and still reluctant acknowledgment of the rights to first-class citizenship for the Negro, in the advent of Medicare for the aged, in Operation Head Start, in more support for educational innovation, in the Peace Corps, and in Vista.

The expansion of human support services will engender still greater demands for additional services and for faster development of those already established. As people begin to

[2] Address by Secretary of Agriculture Orville L. Freeman to the annual meeting of the National Rural Electric Cooperative Association, San Francisco, California, February 22, 1967.

become more educated, healthier, and more politically aware through exposure to the services now being developed, they will demand still more services, pushing their demands with rent strikes, boycotts, protest actions of all sorts, through elections, and, when they deem it necessary, through violence. But as we have begun to learn with the poverty program and with our expanded education programs, designing and implementing these programs, on the one hand, and on the other doing so so that they build on one another, are enormously complex tasks. Programs, personnel, organizational styles, money, politics, and people must be meshed and kept meshed. And these tasks will become more complex as demands grow and the possibilities for alternative services enlarge.

Certainly the most critical domestic area for years to come, so far as this source of complexity is concerned, will be how to produce rapidly the wholesale and stable articulation of our white and black populations into an affluent, highly technologized society. We have done badly to date, and as white and Negro struggle to find—or to avoid—solutions, the situation has become more difficult rather than less. The terror of massive violence and counterviolence looms large in the years ahead.[3] While the Vietnam war contributes to the problem, clearly it isn't the only factor, as is evidenced by school desegregation battles, inequities in wages between

[3] This book is premised on the assumption that somehow the United States will cope with the deepening impasse between black and white human beings in a way that does not destroy our Judeo-Christian heritage in the process. At worst, there is the likelihood of a quick end to our way of life based on the values we claim to cherish. At best, there is no likelihood of a quick end to mutual violence, bitterness, and misunderstanding. At best, then, we are bound to face the kind of world described herein.

comparable jobs held by blacks and whites, resistances to open housing in the suburbs, and violence and threats of violence.

We can expect the large and vocal young population to make its needs heard, and we can expect the increasingly larger, healthier, and earlier retired older population to insist on its needs being met.

We have seen youth in action, desegregating the South, organizing the grape-pickers in California, experimenting with the "turned on" social arrangements of the Hippies, upsetting the multiversity, plaguing communities with riots and horseplay, abroad organizing communities as members of the Peace Corps, at home organizing the poor, doing for marijuana and psychedelics what their generation of the 1920's did for the cocktail party, and, in general, upsetting convention and complicating life for their elders as they search for a meaningful replacement for the "sold-out big system" they repudiate. But for all their impact, socially, stylistically, and as media fare, the socially activist dissident proportion of the younger generation is probably around 10 percent, though no one really knows. Some significant portion of those identified with the "turned-on" community are uninterested in influencing the larger world in which their "dropped-out" life is imbedded. Probably both the activist and dropped-out groups will grow, their numbers being a reflection of the level and kind of turmoil at a given time. Thus, the younger generation of both socially active and dropped-out dissidents will pose ever greater and more difficult demands on society, some of which will be responded to positively, some of which will be punitively, even ruthlessly suppressed. In either case, dealing with the younger generation will become more complex.

As for the 60–65 and older, here too we can expect increased specialized demands for human support services. With more earlier retirements, better health, and larger incomes, and with larger numbers in this age group, more resources and vitality for political action will be available to further their own needs. Since the old represent both different living styles and values and perspectives derived from an earlier time, they will seek different goals than the younger generations, certainly different goals than the population under 25.

Thus, in their different needs and different styles at least, these three groups, the young, the old, the Negroes and other members of what Gunnar Myrdal calls the "underclass," will place on society exceedingly complex social welfare demands that will require very careful allocations of material and psychological resources if they are to be effectively responded to.

Those who feel themselves polluted by water and air, sight and sound, will be heard from more often. And as we are beginning to realize, the newly unionized, particularly the service unions, and particularly those service unions associated with critical public services such as teaching or fire-fighting or social work, have yet to make their full economic and political impact on a complex society that in good part depends on their services in order to cope with complexity.

A fourth contribution to complexity, a direct product of the large size of the population, results in several novel and important consequences: even if the *percent* of events that occur doesn't increase, the *number* of events that occur will increase. An especially important example has to do with the fact that, as more literate and socially active people are produced (simply as a matter of population growth), more information and ideas will be distributed, good, bad, and indifferent, right, wrong, valid and invalid. But this information will still have to be discovered, discriminated, and absorbed through one human brain per person. Formal information can be compacted by data-processing methods. But the day-to-day information about ideas and events comprising people's day-to-day world can't be compacted and still carry the freight of conjecture, implication, and relationship to other information necessary to serve both the emotional and intellectual needs of the alert citizen.

Ideas will not be the only source of increased information to be dealt with. In a highly mobile and communicative society more people result in more things happening; these things will happen more often even if they have a low probability of occurring. One of the world's largest tankers, the *Torrey Canyon*, disintegrating on a reef and decimating the coastal recreation areas of southern England is probably even more unlikely today than it was in the past (given modern navigational aids), but there are more huge tankers today than in the past to which such an unlikely event may happen. In 1966, only 1 percent of the baggage checked with the airlines was mishandled but that 1 percent represented 1.7 million bags! So, too, with regional electric power failures. And so, too, with political assassinations by "madmen," and other strange and horrible crimes. Anticipating and dealing with unlikely events will become an increasingly important but especially difficult task, full of complex operational problems as well as ethical and legal issues of control and responsibility.

As a result of the increase in number of events and increased size of the market, the number of formats through which they are reported will expand: more books, TV channels, magazines, newsletters, pundits, etc. But this increased number of sources reporting on and interpreting the state of man and the universe will not necessarily mean that the interested citizen or professional will have an enlarged and more balanced view of what is "really" happening. First, he will have to know *where* to look, through what sample of information sources, to get an adequate range of interpretations. This will become more difficult to do as the number of information sources increases. But even if he does discover a valid sample of positions, he will then have the difficult task of integrating them to arrive at an informed position based on them. Given the complexity of the issues, and the rapid rate of change in them, and given the assertions of each source that it has the full and balanced picture, that its "exclusives" are the true and full ones, the task of differentiation, discrimination, and integration will become steadily more intricate for those who seek to know and to act on what they know.

Most people, however, will deal with this situation in customary ways: when they pay attention to issues at all, they will assume that their usual sources of information are correct. And most people, under most circumstances, won't pay attention to most issues. Walter Lippmann states:

Because their ideas are out of date while their lives are being changed so rapidly, modern men are driven to concentrate their attention and their energies on working out the detailed consequences of change for themselves and their families. They have become, they have had to become, "pragmatic" in the sense that they deal with the details of living and making a living and have put aside the great world. They do not have the ambition to participate in history and to shape the future. Modern men are predominantly isolationists. They are preoccupied with the more immediate things which may help or hurt them. Their state of mind is marked by a vast indifference to big issues, and in this indifference there is a feeling that they are incompetent to do much about the big issues.[4]

Thus, on the one hand, for those who make and respond to the interplay of issues, the sheer increase in events and ideas will mean increased complexity for them to deal with. On the other hand, complexity will not increase in this way for those who do not in general respond to the larger world. But when particular issues do involve this latter population and they do react to them, their relatively simplistic responses to elaborately interrelated issues will, by that very fact, further complicate matters for those trying to deal with these responses in their more complex setting.

For there is another way to look at the complexity-increasing aspects of large populations: small percents of people represent large absolute numbers of people. In the kind of world we are moving into very small percents of people represent numbers large enough to perturb the conventional conduct of society. For example, the ghetto riots have generated a pall of apprehension resulting in a variety of national responses, including summer hiring programs, more water hydrants, exacerbation of both black-power and white antagonism to civil rights, and a generally touchy and "trigger happy" state of mind in private citizens, city governments, and federal agencies. Other factors contribute to the attention given to riots and threats of riots, such as hostility and anxiety in both opponents and proponents of civil rights

[4] Walter Lippmann, "Today and Tomorrow . . . Catching Up with the Times," *Washington Post*, November 14, 1966.

developments in general, and intensive coverage by the media, especially the impact of TV. But increasingly in the foreground are the anticipated terrible consequences from the number of places and people that could explode, even though the percent of the population involved would still be small.

The demonstration at the University of California Berkeley campus involved only a small percent of the student body, but it continues to send quivers through the conventional administrative processes of higher education, to say nothing of conventional parents, other citizens, and legislators. And it has led to persisting pressures on and some important changes in the relationship between students, teachers, and course content in some schools. We can expect in the future that small percents of people acting collectively to protest this and demand that will, by virtue of their large numbers, increase the likelihood that they will have to be attended to. Thereby they will increase the variety of social action and reaction and in so doing they will further complicate the conduct of society.

Partly deriving from the above sources of complexity, partially independent of them, is another source of complexity: the uneven impact of change. One tends to write of the consequences of the convergencies of technology and other social factors as if the causes and effects were homogeneous, monolithic. Nothing could be less likely. People will differ in manner and degree in their responses to the developments explored herein, and these differences in response will contribute to differences in the consequences of their responses both for them and for others. There will be time differences too, both when people respond and when the feedback from their responses affects others. Combined with the sources of complexity already referred to, these differential responses to change are certain to complicate enormously the conduct of society. Four examples give a feeling for this source of complexity.

One: between the developed nations and the emerging areas of the world there is an increasing gap in comparative ability to exercise social control and technological control of the material environment. Two: at home cybernation has a differential impact on and produces different responses in skilled compared to unskilled workers. This is part of the extensive differential impact of technology and megalopolization on affluent whites compared to poor blacks. Three: there is too little appreciation of the coming differential impact of social engineering on various of our customary political processes and standards. The time spans required for implementing long-range planning and the objectivity required to evaluate programs as they evolve seem incompatible with many conventional political tactics. At its starkest it may well be that, as Harvey Cox suggests, the "urban technologists" and the "participant democrats" are headed for a "collision." [5]

The fourth example of the differential impact of social change deserves more extended comment, being less familiar than the others. The hugeness of this society, its affluence, and its democratic ethos will make it possible for those who have the wits, courage, and will to do so, to experiment with alternatives to the main patterns of living. The Peace Corps and the Hippies represent two such alternatives today. For

[5] Harvey Cox, "Technology and Democracy," *Technology and Culture in Perspective* (Cambridge, Mass.: The Church Society for College Work, 1967), p. 4.

some, these alternatives will be lived in as important educative experiences; for others they will be their "permanent" way of life. In the social interstices provided by megalopolized society, some individuals and groups will choose to live quite differently from the typical pattern, as they make deliberate, differential responses to hugeness, affluence, technology, and bureaucracy. Hunter S. Thompson gives an example of such an ongoing experiment:

. . . despite the fact that the whole journalism industry is full of unregenerate heads, i.e., users of psychedelic agents—just as many journalists were hard drinkers during Prohibition—it is not very likely that the frank, documented truth about the psychedelic underworld, for good or ill, will be illuminated at any time soon in the public prints.

If I were to write, for instance, that I recently spent 10 days in San Francisco and was stoned almost constantly . . . and that nearly everyone I dealt with smoked marijuana as casually as they drank beer . . . and if I said many of the people I talked to were not freaks and dropouts, but competent professionals with bank accounts and spotless reputations . . . and that I was amazed to find psychedelic drugs in homes where I would never have mentioned them two years ago—if all this were true, I could write an ominous screed to the effect that drugs, orgies and freak-outs are almost as common to a much larger and more discreet cross section of the Bay Area's respectable, upward-mobile society as they are to the colorful drop-outs of San Francisco's new Bohemia.

There is no shortage of documentation for the thesis that the current Haight-Ashbury scene is only the orgiastic tip of a great psychedelic iceberg that is already drifting in the sea lanes of the Great Society. Submerged and uncountable is the mass of intelligent, capable heads who want nothing so much as peaceful anonymity.[6]

[6] Hunter S. Thompson, "The 'Hashbury' Is the Capital of the Hippies," *The New York Times Magazine*, May 14, 1967, p. 124.

As with other small percent effects, some alternative ways of life will simply be tolerated by the members of the big society; as with other small percent effects, some life ways may be intensely reacted to by the big society. Either way, these alternative life ways will complicate our world because they will provide events and ideas and circumstances about which decisions will have to be made and actions sometimes taken wherein deeply held values will conflict with each other.

The "interstitial society" phenomenon can be put in more general terms. Earlier I quoted Walter Lippmann's observations about "pragmatic man" who lives in his immediate world because the larger world is changing too fast for him to adjust to. Now there are others, though again a small percent, who not only adjust to rapid social changes but enjoy being involved in them. This range of response to change is what we would expect if the human capacity to learn and unlearn—to adjust to change—can be represented like other attributes, say, along a normal curve of distribution. Certainly there is no reason to suppose that in this characteristic everyone is equally endowed. Then, in a rapidly changing environment some people will be better able to adapt than will others. So, in tomorrow's world of rapid change, we will have, at least at the ends of the continuum, two cultures: one designed for those who enjoy and seek rapid change and one designed for those who are made anxious and inadequate by such rapid change. The life ways of the two cultures will be different, perhaps as different as those that have characterized the affluent compared to the poor. Perhaps, as with poverty in America, for a long time we will pretend the difference really doesn't exist or we will rationalize its existence on some latter-day moral grounds. But as with poverty, one way or another, the difference in capacity to adapt will add new tasks for those trying to evolve the whole society at minimum cost to its parts.

A fifth source of complexity is the likely scale and scope of *unanticipated* impacts from the new, developing, powerful technologies, particularly from automation and computers (i.e., cybernation), social engineering, and biological engineering. Here additional complexity arises because even though our knowledge will be increasing at an unprecedented rate, thereby giving us a greater ability to predict the first-order consequences of the application of new technologies, the very scope and scale of the impacts of these unprecedentedly potent technologies mean that there will be unanticipated secondary and tertiary consequences of perhaps greater importance than the primary ones. A familiar example illuminates this point. The automobile enormously enhanced our control over distance, but perhaps more profoundly it contributed critically to loss of control over the urban environment and to the almost total breakdown in traditional means for controlling adolescent behavior, especially sexual conduct. Certainly running society has become a far more complex task as a result of the automobile.

Turmoil

Turmoil, as a characteristic of the years ahead, can be viewed as an important subcategory under "Complexity." However, it merits a subtitle in this chapter, if only because it is our national characteristic to assume that the future will be better, that today's problems will be worked out by then, and as the semantics of the Great Society suggest, everything will be tranquil or, if not tranquil, at least the turmoil will be more invigorating than disrupting—like recreation. This isn't the way the next couple of decades look to me or to some others.

A British expert on social systems and decision-making sees the next few decades this way:

. . . political and social life is bound, I think, to become much more collectivist or much more anarchic or—almost certainly —both. Communities, national, sub-national and even supranational, will become more closely knit insofar as they can handle the political, social, and psychological problems involved and more violent in their rejections insofar as they cannot. The loyalties we accept will impose wider obligations and more comprehensive acceptance. The loyalties we reject will separate us by wider gulfs from those who accept them and will involve us in fiercer and more unqualified struggles.[7]

The political scientist Hans J. Morgenthau has this to say more specifically,

The restoration of our cities under government auspices implies radical change in the control and the values of real estate. Public mass transportation can only be established at the expense of the private motor industry and its subsidiary industries. The systematic shift of an economy of scarcity to one of abundance, in which the government will provide all with the necessities of life, will shift the gravity of economic power from the private to the public sector.

It is utopian to expect that such a radical transformation of the power structure of American society will be supported by a consensus. It can only be achieved as the result of a series of strenuous and violent social conflicts. These conflicts are likely to

[7] Sir Geoffrey Vickers, "The End of Free Fall," privately circulated mimeograph, p. 21. In revised form in *The Listener*, LXXIV, No. 1909 (October 28, 1965).

produce novel political alignments which will render meaningless the traditional juxtapositions between capital and labor, right and left, conservative and liberal.[8]

Charles Hitch, the economist who developed or directed much of the systems analysis, program-budgeting and planning-systems methods, and other sophisticated procedures for rationalizing the Department of Defense, has said,

. . . I fear that the backlog of demand accumulated during World War II, the heavy military expenditures of the 1950's, and a certain amount of good luck have made us too complacent [about] monetary-fiscal-employment-inflation problems. I for one would be amazed if we did not have some very troublesome depressions in the 1960's, and I am far from convinced that we have the knowledge, institutions, or will to cope with them promptly and adequately.[9]

One source of turmoil in the years ahead will be malfunctions in the social and physical environment that lead to a reverberating set of disruptions. More urban ghetto riots. Or a prolonged national strike of public service personnel. Or a larger-scale version of a thalidomide-type tragedy. Or a showdown between militant black power and equally militant but better armed (with weapons, laws, and media control) white power. Or 500 million dead in one year from famine in Asia. Or years of Vietnam or follow-on wars with our population polarized into those who are furious with

8 Hans J. Morgenthau, "The International Aspects of the Great Society," in Bertram M. Gross (ed.), *A Great Society?* (New York: Basic Books, 1968), p. 107.

9 Charles J. Hitch, "The Uses of Economics," *Research for Public Policy,* Brookings Dedication Lectures (Washington, D.C.: The Brookings Institution, 1961), p. 98.

the non-white enemy and those who are furious with a deceptive and manipulative executive branch of government.

In addition to disruption arising from cumulative sets of circumstances, there will be those sudden disruptions—massive accidents—that in some sense are the result of balancing costs against risks but which still have a more "accidental" character to them. An inversion layer over New York that kills 20 thousand people. The first, second, and third crashes of 500-passenger jumbo-jets. A regional electric power failure that lasts long enough to disorganize rather than just slow down a city—a power failure that occurs, say, during a hot, racially tense summer. The accidental detonation of a nuclear weapon in a heavily populated region.

Not only can one imagine any number of such events but the chances are overwhelming that some of them will happen. When they do, they will also confront pertinent institutions with the kind of personally and organizationally upsetting conditions that provide the most effective conditions for initiating rapid organizational change. Of course, such organizational changes occasion further turmoil within and without the organization.

The problem of evaluating the adequacy and validity of technical knowledge—and more knowledge will become technical, as I shall argue later—in order that individual citizens and contending organizations can act informedly in their own interests will become more difficult. Arguments will become more contentious. For during this period ambiguities and contradictions in "authoritative information" will increase. Those activities that in fact or in image intermix science and technology, especially those scientific-technological activities that also intermix political power, are becoming in-

creasingly partisan: the scientist-technologist's identification
is as much or more with the organization with which he is
affiliated as it is with "science." We can see this evidenced
today in the arguments promulgated by scientist-technicians
about the pros and cons of genetic effects of radioactive fallout from atomic weapon testing; or the utility or lack of it of
shelters for nuclear attack; or whether pesticides are mostly
innocuous or dangerous; or about the consequences of smok-
ing; and in the arguments about the alleged virtues of a supersonic transport or manned space exploration.

As a result of this trend, many who would have assumed
scientific information to be factual and precise information,
"incontrovertible" information, will interpret what is offered
as scientific information to be partisan information instead.
As such it will be subject to cynicism and doubt or downright
rejection. Thus, while "scientific" information could add to
the quality of the arguments, the assumption that it is biased,
even in those cases where in fact the data will be as complete
as knowledge permits, will also complicate resolution of the
arguments because the data will generally not be given the
determinative role they would have if they were accepted as
nonpartisan information. Instead of reducing emotionalism
in public policy issues, "scientific information," to the extent it is rejected by some as "partisan" and insisted on by
others as "objective," may simply deepen antagonisms.

What's more, as institutions become larger and their problems and programs more complex, the public relations shield
behind which they work will become broader and stronger.
Partly because of the vested interests or political power of
those dispensing the information, partly because the technical
knowledge possessed by any citizen will be minuscule on

most matters, and partly because of the ethical and technical complexity of most major issues, what will be communicated to citizens, ostensibly so they can judge their self-interest, will be less and less a representation of all the factors which ought to go into their assessment. This inadequate access to reality is clearly the case already with defense policy, space policy, and economic policy. Even the intelligent and conscientious citizen does not have or cannot decipher the technical information needed to make informed judgments; for example, on the current controversies about the development of new weapons, manned or unmanned space programs, or the real impact of automation. It will increasingly be so with other policies. In part, the information needed won't be provided by those who have it and who will use it selectively for their own ends. In part, there will be no way to judge the validity and sufficiency of the information which is available. More often than in the past, those "outside" will not know what they should be looking for. Whatever the situation "inside," it will always be possible to obscure it "outside" with a public information program which masquerades as unimpeachable information, or which claims that there is more to the situation than is understood or can be revealed. This latter claim may in fact be true. The problem is that it will be more difficult to find out if it is true, and if it is true, what it means in view of ignorance about the nature of the unshared information.

Thus, as the information needed for making informed decisions becomes harder to obtain and more difficult to validate as to its completeness, as well as being harder to understand; and as it becomes more evident that small percents of the population can upset organizations, protest politics, another source of turmoil, will be practiced more. In the years ahead, we shall see many more efforts to influence policies and procedures through activities aimed at circumventing the logical, legal, and bureaucratic processes of government, industry, or service organization. Boycotts, sit-ins, overloading the mayor's telephone switchboard so he can't get calls in, interfering with public events by clogging transportation arteries with "stalled" cars, and so on will be used as negotiating devices by protesting groups that feel themselves otherwise unable to break through the massive, formal operating processes and entrenched viewpoints of big bureaucracies.

Scarcity

Complexity and turmoil will reflect and further increase the scarcity of both skilled manpower and time needed to cope with tomorrow's world. Skills and time will often be in critically short supply. As Kenneth S. Lynn states,

. . . until recently the question of whether our reservoir of potential professionals was going to prove adequate to a constantly growing demand rarely came up. The problem of training more doctors, more lawyers and more engineers was treated as if it were analogous to training more automobile mechanics or welders. Ignoring the difference in intellectual rigor between professional and vocational training, we facilely assumed that if only funds and facilities were made available the nation would call into being as many professionals as it needed. In the summer of 1963, however, the research division of the National Education Association reported that despite all the efforts, particularly in the natural sciences, which have been made to persuade qualified young men and women to enter college teaching, demand has far outrun supply in the fields of mathematics, physics, chemistry, biology, economics, foreign languages (especially Russian), English and engineering. The result is that many colleges and universities have been forced to lower their teaching standards. The report further warned that this situation is getting worse, rather than better. Experts on other callings have also begun to suggest that we are approaching the saturation point in our ability to multiply professional personnel.

Because there are simply not enough professionals to go around, the practitioner of today is perforce burdened with too much work, thereby jeopardizing existing professional standards even further. It is notable how many [concerned with the professional] emphasize the multiplicity of demands that are made on the contemporary clergyman, teacher, doctor and scientist. Administrative demands increasingly divert them from their real work, while demands for their professional services are made not only by an ever expanding clientele, but by business and government, both of which have come to depend upon the advice of professional consultants.[10]

But there is more to the matter than is explicit in this quotation. It will not be enough to produce what we usually think of as occupationally highly skilled people. In order for people to cope with the personal challenges with which the world we are describing will confront them, we will need many people skilled in being human: in warmth and trust, openness and compassion, in being nonmanipulative and nonexploitative. In order to lead, to plan, to govern tomorrow's world, in order that the individual and the ineffable are cherished in a megalopolized, technologicized world, we will need administrators, policymakers, and executives with these characteristics, or at least with the capacity to recognize the desperate importance of these characteristics. We will be

[10] Kenneth S. Lynn, "Introduction to 'The Professions,' " *Daedalus*, XCII, No. 4 (Fall 1963), 651–652.

short of such compassionate men, of men who can appreciate the human condition, who will have the courage to resist either underusing or overusing the unprecedented technological power they will have. Wise men have always been scarce. They'll be relatively scarcer tomorrow because there will be more places where they will be needed if we are to use our technologies and our occupational skills effectively and humanely. As of now, we do not deliberately produce such skilled people; we don't know how. Indeed, I strongly suspect that we are not even sure we want to. The radical changes in the customary conduct of our lives and livelihoods implied by such qualities are very uncomfortable for most of us to contemplate. Thus, both conventionally highly skilled people and those with the needed human skills will be in short supply over the next couple of decades. If we wanted them tomorrow, we should have been training them in the numbers needed yesterday.

Time will be in critically short supply too. Time to build new cities—rather than "slurbs"—and to rebuild old cities, to clean our water and air, to train professionals, to invent new political institutions, to update outmoded organizations, to create new ways to teach and to learn, to control world population, to grow modern societies in emerging areas, to acquire and prepare recreation areas, to eliminate urban ghettos and to gather knowledge from these efforts in order to improve the ways we do them. All these tasks will take years to accomplish, during which period we will have to cope with the consequences of shortages, malfunctions, and inequities, because we didn't start these things years ago and are hardly beginning on most of them today. As such, we will be plagued with social disruptions and inefficiencies that will make our supply of skilled people relatively smaller and the time pressures to get things done all the greater. In the midst of affluence and inspiring examples of what can be done, many people will be impeded and frustrated, emotionally and intellectually deprived, physically and aesthetically assaulted by rancid air, water, and cities. They will be guilt-ridden and hostile with themselves and with others in turn for their inadequacies in dealing with the demands for decency and attention we place on one another.

What human resources and time there will be to meet these backlogged needs will have to be husbanded carefully. Later, we will examine the implications of these shortages for long-range planning.

❧ 3 ❧

THREE PREPOTENT
TECHNOLOGIES

. . . A characteristic of our technology . . . is new, if only because it is today's technology, and not yesterday's. It is that we possess, in absolute terms, far greater physical power and technical capability than ever before. It is not necessary to claim that atomic energy represented a greater change than gunpowder to realize that the atomic bomb is more powerful than TNT. Printing might easily have induced a greater social shock than the computer—it upset the educational monopoly of the Church, for one thing—yet the fact remains that the computer can deal with far more information almost infinitely faster than printing can. In absolute terms, we have far more power than anybody.[1]

In this chapter, we shall examine some aspects of three technologies that have extraordinary implications for the directions society may take over the next twenty years. These are: cybernation, social engineering, and biological engineer-

[1] Emmanuel G. Mesthene. From an address delivered at the American Management Association's Second International Conference and Exhibit, "Educational Realities," New York, August 9–12, 1966.

ing. Here, I will not provide the reader with an inventory of what these technologies can be expected to do. Rather, I want, on the one hand, to draw attention to the less well-recognized potentialities in these technologies for facilitating the attainment of social goals; and, on the other hand, I want to show why it will be necessary to do much more long-range planning than we have heretofore practiced in order that these technologies, operating in and operated on by the social environment earlier described, will not destroy us ideologically, perhaps physically.

Let me begin by asserting that the potentials of these technologies cannot be usefully understood by assuming that they are either the villains or heroes of tomorrow's drama. However, I am not thereby subscribing to the conventional wisdom that technology is neutral and that "it is what society does with it that determines its promise or threat." That proposition was all right in the innocent, gee-whiz, who-knows-what-will-come-of-it, past. It won't do today. For part of our society increasingly, self-consciously *chooses* what technologies to develop for what purposes. Today technology is not just harvested; it's planted too, at great expense and on the basis of sophisticated assessments of likely payoff. Thus, the development of the primary technologies and that of the secondary and tertiary technologies needed in order to apply the primary ones are matters increasingly in need of explicit *social* planning. It is no longer sufficient to assume that either the use of or the development of technology can be pursued in a laissez-faire spirit independently of other values and needs for social growth, stability, or change that may be jeopardized or facilitated by technological development. That mood was appropriate, indeed necessary, in the days when the technologist was akin to the artist, making almost no economic or organizational demands on society and struggling to have his product noticed by a few on the fringes of the larger social system. Today, the situation is the contrary, and just as the free-wheeling *caveat emptor* operations of big business are being transformed by the needs of a more interdependent society, so too we must expect that the same pressures will be applied to science-technology.

I am aware that the issues we face cannot be solved, by and large, through a moratorium on technological development as such, unless we were to change our values and life ways completely. And we would almost certainly need technology to facilitate the change. The social environment that technology has produced is such that we must use more technology to make our environment more humane and fulfilling. I fully expect technology to help deal with the problems the technologies have and will produce. I also fully expect that unless we develop a much deeper appreciation than we now have of the social implications of technology and the desperate need for complementary social inventions, and for more fully human beings, we are very likely to suffer social disruption and individual diminution. The chances of adverse consequences from these technologies might be no higher than for favorable outcomes. But the magnitude of the consequences, favorable or unfavorable, will be so great that if they are unfavorable, they will bring far more serious trouble than did technology in simpler days when it affected fewer people, in a smaller area, over a longer time period. Indeed, the unfavorable consequences could keep us from ever attaining the favorable ones. If one considers the population explosion as a product of biological technology, the urban mess as a consequence of agricultural and automotive technologies, and the always looming threat of societal extinction as a result of nuclear technology, it's clear that we have yet to remove the potentially overwhelming problems the older technologies have produced. While, with the possible exception of nuclear engineering, we could not have our modern world without these other technologies, because of them we may not have our modern world much longer unless we learn to apply and control even these older technologies more rationally, more humanely than we have so far.

Let us consider, then, three technologies that require much more humane control and rational application to humane goals than these others have received.

Cybernation

"Cybernation," the word I derived from Norbert Weiner's word "cybernetics," refers to the application of computers and automation. Since *Cybernation; The Silent Conquest,* [2] some of the issues presented there have become matters of widespread, usually acrimonious, discussion, particularly those matters having to do with the effects of cybernation on the size and composition of the work force. And descriptions of the versatility of cybernation in the manufacture of things and in the manipulation of symbols have become commonplace. Here I want to draw attention briefly to some less appreciated aspects of the longer-range impact of cybernation particularly pertinent for the thesis of this book. These are

[2] Donald N. Michael, *Cybernation: The Silent Conquest* (Santa Barbara, Calif.: Center for the Study of Democratic Institutions, 1962).

the problems of inculcating new skills and new values toward work and education in the displaced, relatively skilled worker, and the problem of growing intellectual separation produced by cybernation between those working creatively with the computers and the rest of the population.

Consider the impact of cybernation on those people who at any given time will have been skilled workers until cybernation displaced them. More and more skilled people will be subject to such displacement. In the blue collar area, there is the steady incursion of numerical control—the control of production machines by computers programmed to do skilled metal work and other fabrication, to alter the form and content of the product in accordance with predetermined inventory and sales data, to do quality checks—i.e., generally to replace the skilled fabricator and inspector. Many skilled white collar workers' days are also numbered. Accountants are being replaced by the multipurpose computer or by computer service available to the organization that doesn't need or can't afford its own computer. While the computer extends the capabilities of the creative person, as described below, it reduces or removes the need for the engineer or designer who merely carries out routine design activities using handbook-type data according to preset rules. Of course, most of what is "designed" is done by this sort of "skilled" activity.

Moreover, as organizations gain experience with more versatile computers, another process begins to take over. Instead of simply replacing a human by a computer, management moves toward reorganizing its whole operation, toward rationalizing the system.

For example, instead of having batteries of human key-punch operators translating information from mailed-in forms to cards, the trend is to have the form come in from the field marked in such ways that the computer can process it directly. Or instead of having personnel and procedures for quality control by human inspection, the numerically controlled production system does its own. (This, of course, also changes the structure and mandate of personnel management.) I expect the same type of rationalizing process to reduce the need for persons to translate technical reports into language the computer can process. If computer translation remains limited and awkward, the very pressing need for quick access to journal and related information will result in a special application of what Herbert Simon in other contexts has called "environmental control." For example, rather than trying to design a fruit-picking machine that discriminated between ripe and unripe fruit and handled them gently, biological technologists developed fruits that ripen simultaneously and are bruise-resistant. So too we will invent a computer-translatable language that those writing for the journals will use. We will learn to write the way the computer can read rather than use the time-consuming and expensive method of using skilled people as a bridge between author and computer.

With cybernation, whole blocks of activity become unnecessary and new ones arise. But these new ones do not necessarily allow easy transfer of people from the old tasks to new ones, nor do they necessarily involve more people *overall*. There may be a work force reduction in-house or there may be a work force increase in-house resulting from the incorporation of tasks formally done outside the organization as a contracted service. It has taken most of the years during which computers have been available to gain the overall ex-

perience needed to design a coherent *system* fusing cyber-
nated equipment and human organizations, so that, together,
the task they perform is more highly rationalized. This trend,
just beginning, should have substantially greater impact in
the years ahead.

Thus, while we are used to the idea that the unskilled will
have a tough time living meaningful work lives if they have
to compete with cybernation, it is also true that many of the
skilled will also live lives subject to disruption from cybernation.

This means that many occupationally skilled adults and
most students preparing for skill-based occupations will have
to change their perception of the relationship between work
and study. Instead of accumulating a repertoire of skills in
school sufficient for a lifetime career, the future student will
have to learn and the future teaching process will have to in-
culcate the expectation that work and education will be a cir-
cular arrangement. The customary middle-class expectation
of a one-way continuity from school to occupation or career
will no longer be realistic. This new expectation of disrupt-
able occupational patterns will produce in some a sense of
threat—who will have the ability to make it through the next
educative round? Others will see it as an opportunity to try
something else and to discover more about themselves.

Education for a vocational skill also faces a new challenge. The purpose of vocational education will have to become that of providing the student with the skills for relearning and unlearning, for social mobility and adaptability, so
that he can socially and occupationally move with the
changes technology, particularly cybernation, produces. But
such skills have been traditionally fostered by a "liberal edu-

cation" or at least by a college or college-directed education. What then will remain the difference, if any, in substance or pedagogy between vocational and college-oriented education?

When we are not fighting wars, we will have to deal with unemployment—which at least one chairman of the President's Council of Economic Advisors now acknowledges to be structural at around 4 percent [3]—by extending years of schooling and advancing retirement to earlier years. Both training for work and education for leisure will put more strains on the education system and require more advanced planning by agencies with the pertinent responsibilities.

Personal support and guidance to help turn occupational disruption due to cybernation into opportunities for choice and growth is only one reason why there will be an increasing need for people skilled in person-to-person relationships. I don't mean the pseudo-personal response that characterizes so much of our commercialized ethos, but rather the kind that involves true rapport between individuals. These roles depend for their effectiveness on the fact of one person's being emotionally in touch with another. They can't be done by machine because it is not so much the "substance" of the relationship, whatever that may mean, as the fact for one person that another *person* cares, or is there, or is sharing, or is helping.

We can expect then the *potential* for more professional roles that are more human; cybernation will do a better job than humans do of being efficient and uninvolved. And the potential will be there, too, for more paraprofessional roles

[3] "Ackley, in Shift, Ties Job Gain to Training," *The New York Times,* October 27, 1966.

as aids to the professionals and as suppliers of skilled services in everything from baby-sitting, to mother's helpers, to aids to the emotionally and socially dispossessed. But first,

. . . our society must come to recognize the need for such roles and express this recognition through the bestowal of status. We are beginning to do so as evidenced by the Peace Corps volunteer, the teacher's aide, the neighborhood worker in the poverty program, and so on. But the society as a whole has not recognized the need with a sense proportionate to the actual need foreseen by those looking ahead. In particular, many professions persist in maintaining an egregious possessiveness about every aspect of their activities and a most unbecoming superiority about the prerequisites for competence. This makes it exceedingly difficult, often impossible, to establish the needed occupational roles.[4]

The computer is increasingly used to design and to simulate. In the words of the Swedish expert Borje Langefors,

Computers have developed designs that range from airplanes to architecture, from electrical circuits to clothing, from ship hulls to highways. The results have exhibited the constraints of an experienced human designer's feel for form and aesthetics and his canny knowledge of the possibilities and limitations of production facilities . . . [in the future] designers will design the designing system which designs the actual objects.[5]

Using computers whose sensing mechanism looks like a television screen, a designer can sketch on it with a beam of

[4] Donald N. Michael, Paper in "Proceedings of the New England Regional Conference on Education, New England Board of Higher Education," May 19–21, 1966.
[5] Borje Langefors, "Automated Design," International Science and Technology (February 1964), pp. 90–97.

light what he has in mind. The sketch, along with other information about the object (such as building code regulations, tensile strengths, costs per ton), is fed to the computer. The computer "cleans up" the sketch, displays the object from different perspectives, and displays operating information and costs and other criteria pertinent for judging acceptability. For example, a bridge design can be accompanied by figures showing the loads on the various members of the bridge as a function of total load on the bridge. Thus, as the computer varies the total load the designer can watch the variation in load on the supporting members and variations in cost for differing load limits. Previously worked out designs can be stored in the computer's memory so they can be reviewed for their possibilities in varying design tasks.

Another example of computer-as-designer will extend our sense of what the implications are for those who would work at routine "skilled" tasks in the future. Assume a road is to be built through the mountains. Instead of surveyors going into the mountains to measure grades and angles or instead of humans laboriously deriving one road from their reading of aerial stereoscopic photographs of the terrain, the computer does the "designing." It reads the aerial photographs and displays on paper or screen the roads that can be put through the mountains that meet previously specified criteria of grade, cost per mile, and so on.

When using a computer to design, the operator is exploring the potentials of known properties of things and processes whether it be a bridge or an inventory-control system or automatic bakery. In simulation situations the user is trying to develop a model of process that will act the "same" way as the observed "real life" process does. Thus, we try to simulate the operations of the economy or the behavior of public opinion or the outcome of a military strategy or the flight of a yet-to-be-built aircraft or the flow of traffic or the heuristic, problem-solving methods of man or an investment strategy for a nation or corporation. (Out of successful simulations come models that can be used for designing; for example, economic planning strategies, opinion-manipulation procedures, problem-solving computers, and better highway traffic-control systems.) To simulate things in process the computer operator invents and programs the computer with a logical model that states the suspected relationships among variables in the model. The model is then fed data that characterize the expected numerical values the variables will take along with data which represent the environment that the model is supposed to deal with. The output from the simulation describes how this model responded to the particular environment to which it was exposed. For example, how does a public vote when faced with certain choices? Or how does a plane respond to atmospheric turbulence? Or what happens to the GNP if taxes are reduced by X percent? Whether or not the simulation is a good one depends on how congruent the output from the computer is with the significant reality as perceived by the technologist and his clients.

Thus, in neither design nor simulation need the user be restricted to a single "best" output from the computer. The computer produces sets or envelopes of solutions depending on the criteria for acceptable or desirable outputs that it is supplied with. Since these outputs are produced for a human purpose, the criteria of acceptability must reside in the human user. Ultimately, which output alternative is chosen depends on the user's values. Whether one seeks to cut costs, improve reliability, save time, enlarge capacity, make life easier—whatever the form of the quest for a "bigger bang for a buck"—the ultimate choice from among the solutions the computer offers has to be a value-based one. The user can, of course, pretend—or truly believe—that he has no choices beyond those contained in the envelope of alternatives provided by the computer, as defined by his initial selection of *a* preferred-outcome criterion. But since the preferred-outcome criterion is value-based, the computer can provide other choices if the user will change his outcome criterion.

The computer, used wisely, increases the options from which the user can choose. But this increase in options comes at the cost of increased complexity; the computer developed the options by operating on subtle design or simulation models which in turn dealt with a vast variety of alternative inputs. These models allow the user to explore many more contingencies and probabilities than would be possible if the computer didn't exist. But it means that the decision-maker has much harder decisions to make because he *has* to consider much more information—it's there to *be* considered—and much more sophisticated information at that.

Computers used as design and simulation facilitators will produce a new level of knowledge in which definitions of social and material reality will be as unfamiliar as is the world of quantum mechanics compared to the common-sense world of Newtonian physics, and as difficult to convey to the uninitiated as it is to express the cosmopolitan person's world to a member of a nonliterate society.

The creative computer-user increasingly can live in close rapport with this extension of his memory and his logical abilities. Through the multiple-access computer, shared with many human colleagues, he has instant access to the "library" of stored visual, aural, and printed displays and procedures, to the up-to-the-minute thinking of his colleagues, and to the computerized symbols they are using to think with. Already this is producing a new kind of "invisible college." For such a computer-user, thinking independently or thinking along with others will be more effective because one can have much faster access to the thoughts for others working on the same problem. More important, perhaps, one will have quicker access to the consequences of one's own thoughts. Punching a middle-of-the-night hunch into a bedside terminal of a distant computer and getting the results back in moments, to sleep on further, should be a more productive way of thinking in some cases than writing down the hunch and waiting for morning to work it out at the computer center. And it should be far more productive than the results produced when one has to delay the next step in one's thought processes until the step is worked out by hand with no computer assistance.

This rapport with the computer, which will make it possible for the creative person to think in terms of many, many variable, probabilistic, and dynamic relationships, is bound to produce multi-variable, probabilistic, dynamic models of the world that couldn't be invented or evaluated otherwise. And because the thinking will be done in a different environment—the computer-assisted environment—it will produce new types of concepts appropriate to that environment that are not perceivable in other simpler environments. This reconceptualizing that results from man living in a different environment is evident now in the world of high-energy physics, with its reality of photographic records of nuclear-particle tracks and bevatron accelerators, and in biology in its environment of quantum mechanical biochemical process measurements and X-ray diffraction-pattern pictures of protein molecules. This will also come to be the case in the behavioral sciences as the behavioral scientist lives in his computerized environment of many variable dynamic representations of social reality.

Gradually then, in all areas where logical model-building can enhance our understanding of social and material reality, we can expect the computer to enable men to create descriptions of that reality that will be essentially incomprehensible to those who are not part of the world where reality is mediated by the computer. For example:

The mathematical economists are apparently winning out over their less quantitative brethren both here and in Moscow—in a decade or two, for example, it may seem incredible that men once thought of the difference between capitalism and Communism as the clash between Adam Smith's freedom and Karl Marx's collectivism. In that more sophisticated era, the difference between the two systems may be widely recognized as the contrast between, say, Jones's system of non-linear difference-differential equations with invariant parameters as against Petrov's matrices, all of whose elements are stochastic variables entering into a Markov chain. Then the controversy would be in such a rarefied atmosphere that nobody could understand it well enough to get passionate about it. A comforting thought in this thermonuclear era.[6]

As we shall see, living with these new realities will pose formidable problems for leadership and citizenship in a democracy. Thus, it is that C. P. Snow observes:

[6] "Mathematics and Economics," Editorial, *The New York Times,* May 2, 1965.

. . . one can't help brooding over the cybernetic revolution which is now breaking over us—the revolution which is being caused by the new sources of information and control, the computers whose effect (and whose putative nature) we are only partially beginning to understand. One thing stands out as a warning and as a hope. This is going to be the biggest technological revolution men have known, far more intimately affecting men's daily lives, and, of course, far quicker, than either the agricultural transformation in Neolithic times or the early industrial revolution which made the present shape of the United States. To understand the actual technique of this cybernetic jump, we shall need deep and original conceptual minds. . . . This means that mathematicians—or, more exactly, any men and women of mathematical insight—are going to take on a new relevance in all advanced societies.[7]

Social Engineering

Social engineering is the systematic application of knowledge and theory about men and institutions to the guidance-transformation-manipulation of men and institutions. Relatively primitive social engineering is used in a variety of contexts today. One example is the application of learning-theory models to the design of programmed instruction, perhaps most familiarly and impressively represented in the computerized machines for teaching reading, pioneered by Omar Moore. Another is the often successful reorganization of management and administration procedures in businesses and government offices based on the research-derived theories and practices about productive relationships between individual motives, group processes, and management goals as developed by such behavioral scientists as Chris Argyris,

[7] C. P. Snow, "Government, Science, and Public Policy," *Science*, CLI (February 11, 1966), 652–653.

Warren Bennis, Robert Kahn, and Rensis Likert. Human-engineering methods have revolutionized the design of complex man-machine environments from giant earth movers to space capsules. Planned social-change techniques, such as those being developed by Ronald Lippitt, to introduce innovations in teaching methods are yet another example. Operation Head Start got much of its technical stimulus and, to an arguable extent, its direction from the work of Martin Deutsch and his associates on the effects of a deprived early environment on childhood learning. Community-action philosophy as initially promulgated in the poverty program derived from research on the role of community processes in frustrating or stimulating personal and community growth. The new emphasis on community mental-health techniques derives from similar studies and experience. As the ill-famed government-sponsored Project Camelot evidences, we are intent on developing the information and theory to apply social engineering to the manipulation of other societies.[8] Of course, there is the application of public-opinion theory and data to the analysis and influencing of public opinion. And there is the application of Keynesian-type theory to the economy, and the application of various behavioral theories to market research.

Thus, we already are using social engineering. There are reasons, however, for believing that in the future the use of social engineering will be much more widespread and the tools and techniques much more potent than at present. In addition to further refinement of the research methods that have led to present applications there are new developments

[8] This research program studied the conditions affecting political stability and instability in politically volatile nations.

that will enhance the knowledge and theory available for expanding extant social-engineering applications and for developing new ones.

One such development overlaps biological engineering and it will be discussed there: the application of chemical and electrical techniques for obtaining a deeper understanding of emotional and cognitive processes.

Another new tool now being fashioned is that of "social accounting": the development of quantitative and qualitative measures for describing the quality and quantity of individual and group life in order to provide information about what cultural and welfare resources people have access to, what resources they need, and how they are responding to their circumstances. Such information will be analogous to that now available with regard to the economy and will be used for planning, operating, and evaluating social policy as we now plan and evaluate economic policy. The extent to which social accounting indices can be formulated and applied depends in good part on the existence of the computer, probably the most important single tool for extending the sophistication and application of social engineering over the next years.

For the computer provides the social scientist with two conditions he has always needed and never had in order to develop a deep understanding of and powerful technology for altering social processes. The computer provides him with the means for combining in complex models as many variables as he needs in order to simulate the behavior of men and institutions. Previously the behavioral scientist simply could not deal with as many important variables as are needed to understand and predict much of human behavior.

From now on he will increasingly be able to do so. (Not everything that is important about human beings can be so formulated. However, much that is important can be put in these terms, enough to bring about substantial improvements in our ability to understand and predict and, hence, control behavior.)

In additon to the capability to build enormously complex models which simulate "real life" behavior of men and institutions, the social scientist can for the first time test these models against the actual social world. For the computer, through its enormous capacity for collecting and processing data, can tell us what is happening to the society today, not—as has usually been the case with our data about society—what was happening five or ten years ago. Urban data banks containing police records, land-use patterns, demographic information, electric-power load distribution, tax records, and so on are already in operation in several cities. Election night is another demonstration of the new capability of social engineering, of what's to come. Data from around the nation are collected and processed so rapidly that very good forecasts of the outcome of elections are available before the West Coast polling places close. The extraordinary accuracy of these computer forecasts derives from extraordinarily complex simulation models within the computer that evaluate the incoming data on the bases of both past voting patterns and many field and laboratory-derived formal models of what factors operating on what groups will affect voting behavior in what ways.

Thus, the social engineer not only can know the state of society now as represented by these data, but he can use them to test and refine his theoretical models in ways analogous to those used in refining simulation models that describe the behavior of rockets, aircraft, etc.

Two particularly pressing social tasks will provide special incentives for developing another kind of knowledge that will greatly increase the potency of social engineering. The tasks are: (1) to develop really effective methods for facilitating early education and especially early education for deprived children; and (2) to transform poor people into middle-class Americans. (Like it or not, this latter goal seems to be what the poverty program is aimed at.) But to accomplish these tasks we need far more knowledge than we now have of the long-term processes that produce individual and social change as a result of interactions between the person and his changing social and material environment.

In other words, we need many longitudinal studies. We have had a few such studies in the history of the social sciences and they have been very valuable indeed. Terman's study of gifted children comes readily to mind, as do some of Margaret Mead's studies on cultural changes over time in her Manus subjects. Nevertheless, though longitudinal studies are crucial for the development of really powerful social science and social technology, they have not been done for the most part. Inadequate data processing and data-storage technology have been two reasons. Additionally, the means for attaining recognition and funds in the scholarly world have militated against such studies: promotions and reputation depend on frequent publishing, and fund sources gain much of their repute (or at least those who dispense the funds do) from the publications, promotions, and empires of their "clients." But with growth in the numbers of social engineers, in research funds, public attention to social issues, and computers, this picture will change in the years ahead, and increasingly this new source of highly revealing knowledge will be available for setting programs and purposes and establishing the means for attaining and evaluating them.

As with hardware technologies, there is an inevitable multiplier in social technologies too. The applications of physical technology have accelerated as the knowledge and experience gained at earlier stages of the technology's development have multiplied the capability to produce newer and more powerful physical technologies. The 2,500-fold increase in about two decades in the power of nuclear weapons and, in about half as many years, the growth in the size of rocket payloads from a grapefruit's diameter to a three-man capsule are two outstanding, though by no means unique, examples of the result of systematically building on accumulated knowledge. We can expect the same accelerating process to operate in the social-engineering area. As we shall see later, the opportunity and the need to expand social engineering will also increase as a result of the requirements for longer-range planning technology.

Biological Engineering

Biological engineering is the application of knowledge to the manipulation of man's biological self and his biological environment. As with cybernation and social engineering, this is not a completely new activity. Aspirins, contraceptives, tranquilizers, pesticides, antibiotics, and metal bone replacements have been with us for some time, and electronic heart pacers and artificial kidneys, while much newer, are definitely a practicable part of biological engineering. But as with the other two technologies, things to come in biology presage profound confrontations for the conduct of society and for the purposes and processes of education. And, in the case of biological developments, it is generally agreed that over the next couple of decades the most dramatic expansion in scientific understanding will be in biology, corresponding in seminal and radical developments to physics during the early decades of the twentieth century. The product of *that* understanding can be symbolized by the release of nuclear energy. An equivalent accomplishment very likely will be the product of the anticipated flowering of biological knowledge.

In the case of biological engineering, the ethical issues that arise take on a special intensity. In part, this will be because many of the issues devolve about one's own body, one's self, or that of a person one is close to, perhaps loves. This "immediacy" is in contrast to the typical impacts of cybernation and social engineering, which tend to be perceived as "out there"; even one's job tends to be dissociated to some extent from oneself. In part the intensity of these ethical issues will be the result of our very modest experience in living with and working through these issues. We have no real experience in many of these biological areas on which to base a widely shared position or even alternative positions on what should be the limits of the acceptable or desirable, compared to the experience we draw on when we are confronted with issues related to economic costs and benefits or free speech or the right to work. What experience we have had is mostly associated with illness, wherein the person on whom biological engineering is practiced is in a submissive relationship: our ethics and behavior have been worked out around the image of the wise doctor or parent who knows best. In cases where this sick-submissive role has not been operative our ethical consensus and agreed-on behavior have been much less well worked out as, for example, in deciding who is entitled to contraceptives and what risks are acceptable when using pesticides. Many of the coming developments fall more in this category. Many of the most significant coming applications in biological engineering carry a heavy freight of two interdependent questions: under what circumstances will use be permissible or mandatory; and who is to have access to the use of a particular development?

Profound long-range planning issues reside in the particular resolution of these questions, and deep insight into the ethical issues and their modes of resolution will be required of both planners and those "planned for." Our planning methods are inadequate and our people, leaders and private citizens alike, are inappropriately educated as of how to cope with these questions. The mood of my concern is reflected in the observations of Dean F. Davies, M.D.:

If a government decides first that a family should be limited to two or three children; second, begins specifying which two persons with similar recessive genes should not mate (sterilization, optional or mandatory, is now legal in some states); and finally, which positive eugenic combination would be best for society; the biologic family will be replaced by one with foster parents. "Once sex and reproduction are separated, society will have to struggle on the one hand with defining the nature of interpersonal relationships which have no long-term social point other than the satisfaction of the individuals concerned; on the other hand, it will have to seek new ways to insure the reasonable care for infants and children in an emotional atmosphere which lacks biological reenforcement through basic sexual and parental drives . . . application of the principle of foster homes on a much

wider scale" will require "a far higher degree of moral sophistication than the average person is likely to possess." [9]

Let us review some of the likely developments in biological engineering, again not in terms of the technologies as
such, but rather with attention to the issues they raise about
use and access to use and the consequent need for long-range
planning.

Electrical stimulation *in utero* seems to produce a more
vigorous and responsive offspring. Whether this works for
humans too remains to be seen; it's being researched now. If
it does work the treatment will cost money, and it will require
some sophisticated interest by the parents-to-be if they are to
know about the process and arrange for its use. As with med-
ication in general, it will probably be the better educated who
use it the most. In this case, however, differential use of *in
utero* stimulation would lead to still a greater gap between
the poor child (from a less well-educated background and,
hence, less likely to have had the advantages of *in utero* stimulation) and the well-educated, usually middle-class, child.

There will be increasing use of organ transplants, organ
replacements, and organ malfunction compensators (such as
the electronic heart pacer). The chances are that for the most
part these will be in short supply (as with the artificial kidney
machine) and expensive. Who gets them by what priority criteria? Ability to pay? Women and children first? Value to the
nation? And the government's role will, of course, be ques-

[9] Dean F. Davies, M.D., Preparatory paper for "National Consul-
tation on Technology and Human Values," Committee on the Church
and Economic Life, Department of Social Justice, Division of Christian Life and Mission, National Council of the Churches of Christ
in the U.S.A., May 2–4, 1967. The quotation within the quotation is
from Robert S. Morison, "Where Is Biology Taking Us?" *Science,*
CLV, No. 3761 (January 27, 1967), 431.

tioned with respect to each development in biological engineering. Since the government right now supports much of the research that will lead to such developments, it could be argued that the government is morally obligated to assume an active role from the beginning, rather than leaving these matters to be worked out in the marketplace or after a thalidomide-type tragedy such as one which may yet reside in the long-range consequences of the initially untrammeled and unexamined application of pesticides.

Promising research is under way on chemicals that appear to improve memory in aged (but not senile) people. Other chemicals appear to be able to erase memories. There is research under way on agents to increase alertness and facilitate learning. And LSD and marijuana are only the most publicized forms of an endless variety of natural and man-made chemical agents that alter emotional states.

To date, outcries against the use of psychedelic agents smack more of prohibitionist rationalizing than of scientific evaluations. What the actual degree of danger for a given person is from such agents is moot, of course, since no one knows how many of what kinds of people are taking how much of which agent.[10] For young people, the danger from

---

[10] Since this was written it has been discovered that LSD produces some broken chromosomes. As of now, there is no clear evidence as to whether and under what circumstances these chromosomal breaks do damage to the user or the offspring of LSD-takers; geneticists differ in their expectations. This is simply another case of our ignorance about the longer-range consequences of the drugs we use. Caffeine and aspirin also break chromosomes. And there are arguments about whether the accumulating DDT in all of our livers will result in long-term damage for the race. Just who has the right to what as between the voluntary ingestion of LSD and the involuntary ingestion of DDT typifies the legal-ethical-technological issues of the next decades.

some agents may be no greater than what they are exposed to while driving under the influence of alcohol or just driving in the exuberant and distracted manner that seems to result in a high proportion of highway accidents in the younger age bracket. And nonaddictive marijuana does not lead to indulgence in the vicious, addictive drugs or to the hostile and destructive behavior so often associated with alcohol. My purpose here is not to argue for or against the use of such agents, but rather to demonstrate that the nature of present responses to psychedelic agents implies an unresolved set of moral, ethical, and legal issues that have to be faced.

These chemicals are easy to buy and in some cases easy to make. Indeed, some who use them are so desirous of sharing with others what they feel to be a wonderful experience that they give them away. More people are using these chemicals, some to expand their sense of self and universe, some to reject what they perceive to be the bureaucratized, commercialized, dehumanized world that surrounds and invades them. And they are being used by people at every occupational and social level. As such, no blunt application of conventional drug-control methods is likely to be workable.

These two factors suggest two critical issues for planning and for education: If these chemicals do provide a rewarding and unique enrichment for some people that is then reflected in a greater ability to live their lives and fill their roles in a complex world, should special provisions be made for them in order to facilitate access to these experiences? The top executive? The minister? The general? The scientist? The poet? On the other hand, if these chemicals become increasingly popular because they enable people to drop out and stay out of the complex world that still needs to be directed—at least long enough to devise means to transform this complex world into some other mode of operating and valuing—then what is to be the position of that part of society that opts to "stay in" with regard to those that "opt out"? As pointed out earlier, an affluent, complex, huge, and relatively permissive society can afford much social experimentation in its interstices—indeed, it can't very well stop it. Will we then have two interlaced societies operating by different values for different ends? If so, how are the decisions to be made about mutual responsibilities of one toward the other and what would be the courts of last resort?

The researches of Penfield, Olds, and Delgado have demonstrated that electrical stimulation of the brain through implanted electrodes can induce sheer terror or ecstatic pleasure, and behavior can be controlled, new behavior taught, and memories repetitively elicited. Of course, these methods probably will be used in the service of evil power to transform, punish, or reward people. Presumably these means simply extend the variety of devices available for coercion or seduction. The *new* ethical issues arise over involuntary submission to purposes established by "enlightened" power, on the one hand, and, on the other hand, over the voluntary use of these methods for giving or receiving pleasure. Who is to decide whether or not to use such devices to retrain antisocial behavior into more acceptable forms? If we have the capacity to retrain quickly and permanently in this way, then the question of what is "antisocial" becomes much more pressing simply because we will know we can, in fact, change the behavior. Who decides then what is antisocial behavior and who decides when it must be changed? Is the politician who bases his campaign on the right to self-induced "electro-pleasure" at safe and sanitary electrode-imbedding emporia to be seen simply as a purveyor of a latter-day version of a chicken-in-every-pot? Or will the grand prize in a commercial come-on be an hour of "Pleasure-Plus" instead of an all-expense tour of New York's night life? In a huge, affluent, pleasure-seeking society of the sort we seem to be becoming, who's to stop such things and why stop them? Surely many will argue the many sides of these questions—and many will do as they wish regardless of where the weight of opinion or law enforcement lies. What then?

In his introductory remarks, as chairman of a day-long symposium on brain biochemistry and mental processes at the 1965 annual meeting of the American Association for the Advancement of Science, the distinguished psychologist David Krech said,

I need not spell out for you what . . . understanding of the mind may mean in terms of the control of the mind. And as soon as I utter that embarrassing science fiction phrase, "control of the mind," you immediately know what is on my mind: the problem of ethics and politics and the social good. Who of us has begun to think seriously of all of these problems? If we should find effective mind control agents who will or should control the mind, control the agents? Should the manufacture and the dispensing of such agents be left to private enterprise or military control or political control? And how should this be done and when and by whom? I don't believe I am being melodramatic in suggesting that what our research may discover may carry with it more serious implications than the awful, in both senses of the word, achievements of the atomic physi-cists.[11]

The ethical issues yet to be worked out, resulting from our growing ability to keep the body alive when it is no longer

[11] Copy of opening remarks supplied in personal correspondence.

human to itself or others, is too evident to merit other than mention here. So too with the issues surrounding the use of nonlethal chemical and biological weapons in warfare. It is worth remarking, however, that the issue goes beyond traditional warfare as such: two weeks of diarrhea would seem to be more humane (and perhaps serve better than bullets) the missions of international police and pacification agencies such as the United Nations. Obviously, other ethics, other values as well as ours will be involved in working this issue through.

There are two other developments likely from biological engineering which, as practicable technologies, are unlikely to face us in the next couple of decades. However, during this time we will be becoming more aware that we will have to face up to the accomplished facts eventually, and such will be the magnitude of their likely impact that systematic attention will have to be given to planning for them long before they arise.

Genetic engineering will be the result of one effort; the deliberate alteration of the molecules that bear inherited characteristics, in order to add or remove characteristics inheritable by subsequent generations. The dialogue has already begun and the basic issues are obvious and almost certainly familiar to anyone reading this.

The other accomplishment will be to extend life-span substantially. But who are to be the first to have this extension, and by what criteria is one's access to this "privilege" to be determined? And who can be permitted to have it in view of the huge world population? What can one do with a longer life, and is one free to terminate it at will? How is power and tenure to be allocated as between the "younger" and the "older"?

The point here is that these accomplishments will come about at least in good part because at some point in the accumulation of knowledge and theory the possibilities will come to appear feasible enough to whoever finances such research to provide the status and funds to carry them to realization. Probably the beginning of such specific developmental work will occur during the period we are concerned with. Possibly it is already under way. On what grounds are decisions to be made to support such research? Or not to support it? Of profound importance, what *other* commitments to seeking knowledge and transforming society must be made at the same time if we want to be prepared to cope with the consequences?

The coincident and related explosions of human population and of biological knowledge may conceivably represent the most critical stage in human evolution since the last great ice age. The ability and necessity to control the numbers and hence (in some respects) the genetic characteristics of future populations could create a situation without precedent in human existence. And, in addition, the availability and refinement of chemopsychiatric drugs suggests both hoped for and frightening possibilities for the manipulation and control of human behavior. Never before have the necessity and the possibility of control over man occurred at so decisive a conjunction.[12]

[12] Lynton K. Caldwell, "Biopolitics: Science, Ethics, and Public Policy," *The Yale Review,* LIV, No. 1 (October 1964), 8.

❧ 4 ❧

ON THE CHANGEOVER TO
LONG-RANGE PLANNING

IN THIS CHAPTER we will begin to explore aspects of a profound societal crisis in the making: our growing intention to undertake long-range planning and our unpreparedness to do it well. A recapitulation is in order first. We are moving into a world of unprecedented scale and complexity. Increasingly, we will have available technologies of unprecedented power for manipulating both the world and men. Our limited experience with such a world and with so much power means we will need more wise men and more time than we will have for them to use their wisdom to deal with the unavoidable challenges that world imposes. Whatever else is abundant, time and skilled humanity will be scarce. But we can no longer afford to let things "work themselves out," to bumble through. The consequences from bumbling into disasters will be too great and the chances of getting out of them while preserving a democratic ethos too small to risk such an approach.

66

The logical and humane direction then would seem to be toward long-range planning in order to anticipate our critical problems and opportunities, to assign to them social priorities, and then to husband our resources in order to meet them. Given what needs to be accomplished through such planning and given the resources we can expect will be available over the next couple of decades, I am led to conclude that if there is any chance of succeeding in coping with our societal needs it will require radical and wide-ranging, coordinated, institutional changes. However, attaining these radical institutional forms and values requires knowledge about how to invent the institutions and circumstances that *in turn* would make possible both the establishment of these institutions and the assignment of appropriately prepared men to undertake the widespread application of longer-range planning itself. But we won't get the knowledge we need as fast as we need it to accomplish this two-step process. The result will too often be bad and dangerous planning or too little planning. For good planning requires sophisticated theory and data about society and appropriate means for applying both, and all three preconditions will take time to attain—during which time we are very likely to be in very serious trouble. The result of this will be more turmoil and complexity and, thereby, still greater need for more and better long-range planning. Here we will examine some socio-psychological problems associated with the circumstances and processes of the *changeover* to long-range planning. For these problems will shed further light on the role of education in such a world.

At this point, a more specific sense of what I mean by planning is needed. I do not mean by "planning" the all too frequent exercise of simply drawing up a set of diagrams and recommendations for what a particular situation should be like five or twenty years from now. These impressive documents almost always end up filed away and, if used at all, they merely serve as rhetorical, almost ritualistic, props for other purposes. Planning, as it is referred to here, does include such diagrams and recommendations, but it also involves planning and vigorous participation in the development and use of the *means* for attaining the recommended ends. (Note that such a definition automatically includes the option, though not the necessity, of "participant democracy" in which those planned for also engage in the planning.) Since the ends will inevitably be modified by the means and by circumstances not anticipated by or beyond the control of the planners, the ends cannot be too rigid or singular in their specification. This means that planning never stops: it is always dependent on evaluations of how things are going according to plan and how things are going outside of the plan, and it is always responsive to the ongoing evaluation of the degree of mesh between the two.

What is the present developing mood about long-range planning? We must go back a bit to better understand it.

Beginning in the 1930's, and especially since the end of World War II, there has been a slow but growing recognition of the need for and capability of planning the opportunities and circumstances for social growth. To fight the great depression and World War II, we were compelled to invent and apply social technologies and hardware technologies on an increasingly large scale. For the most part, until very recently, these efforts at planning the direction of society in order to meet desired goals or to deal with anticipated circumstances were sporadic responses to ongoing crises, and were relatively short-ranged and short-lived. Banfield and Wilson conclude that until after World War II probably no city in the United States was significantly influenced by a master plan.[1]

Techniques for planning and implementing the plans were primitive. There were, and still are, but to a lesser degree, strong and politically effective resistances to such planning by government. There was little appreciation in most of the electorate and in most centers of political power that increasing numbers of social issues were becoming so complex and so large in scale that coherent efforts based on a five-to-twenty-year future perspective were needed to deal with them. But in the last few years the trends toward long-range planning have increased and the indications are that they will accelerate.

There is increasing awareness in political centers as well as among private citizens that many critical social issues will require long-range planning to deal with them; that there are available or potentially available improved techniques for planning and implementing plans; and that it takes time to develop and apply both techniques and end products in order to accomplish the goals to be met through long-range planning.

Consider, for example, the November 27, 1966, statement of Samuel J. Kearing, Sanitation Commissioner of the City of New York, after the three-day incinerator shutdown during that city's air pollution alert:

---

[1] Edward C. Banfield and James Q. Wilson, *City Politics* (Cambridge, Mass.: Harvard University Press, 1965), p. 190.

This crisis has underlined more dramatically than anything we might have said the urgency of adjusting not only city policy but also habits of the public to the problems facing modern cities. Not enough planning has been done to enable the city administration to deal effectively with the mounting problem of waste and pollution. Nor have adequate measures been taken to anticipate emergencies such as the one caused by the dust carrying haze over New York.

The New York Times goes on to report that Mr. Kearing

wants a team of experts in urban development to begin drafting plans now how to modernize the city's garbage disposal system, which will be obsolete within eight or twelve years.[2]

But parallel with a growing awareness that effective human services and a viable environment can only be attained through long-range programs, there is

. . . the very marked tendency for past or existing vested interest to dictate the allocation of resources on the basis of their internal needs . . . national policy is formed from the contention of special interest. Defense industries claim special skills in the solution of poverty problems, health interests would solve problems of regional planning, educators can do anything. All of these forces then tend to produce segmental programs whose cumulative irrationality and need for coordination and comprehensive planning becomes progressively more urgent.[3]

The growing, if limited, appreciation of the need for long-range planning and the empire-building proclivities of government agencies have led to executive action aimed at be-

[2] *The New York Times*, November 27, 1966.
[3] William L. C. Wheaton, "Social Planning: The Incentives and the Constraints," unpublished address at the conference on "The Future of Urban Civilization," University of Wisconsin, January 29, 1966.

ginning to do the needed rationalizing of activities within agencies and among them. Under Secretary McNamara, the Department of Defense, with great effort and mixed if singular successes, was able to bring relatively unprecedented order to its interservice house and to plan much more rationally the nation's long-range national security needs. The planning techniques of program planning and budgeting systems (PPBS) were relatively so much more effective than the previous ad hoc approaches of the separate services that President Johnson, on August 25, 1965, issued a directive to most other executive agencies to apply PPBS and related long-range systematic planning procedures to their efforts. These techniques require the analysis and comparison of costs and benefits for alternative integrated programs that are designed for the purpose of meeting specified, long-range goals. Similar approaches, some using computerized data banks, are sporadically and cautiously being applied in some urban situations by forward-looking managers and governors. Whether these techniques will work well in the agencies and on the human problems to which they are now beginning to be applied will take some years to discover.

In Congress too there are beginnings of awareness that there are too few resources and that it takes too much time simply to expect to deal with bits and pieces of the complex issues of society as they arise. "Crash programs" are increasingly recognized as inherently ineffectual for dealing with basic social goals. An especially significant development is the interest, beginning in 1966–1967, of several senators and representatives in supporting proposals for new planning-pertinent legislation. For example, Senator Edmund Muskie proposed the establishment of a Select Senate Committee to undertake studies of the anticipated impact of technology on the human environment over the next fifty years. Senator Walter Mondale proposed a "Full Opportunity and Social Accounting Act" to insure that both the economic and social costs and benefits are taken into consideration in developing and implementing legislation aimed at goals represented by the "Great Society" idea. Senator Nelson proposed legislation to insure the application of systems analysis and other rationalizing processes to the implementation of social legislation. Representative Emilio Daddario has proposed a Technology Assessment Board. These proposals have been endorsed by several other senators and representatives. More or less the same men endorse each of these proposals, and they represent only a small fraction of the House and Senate. Thus, the present level of support is small. Congress as a whole has a long way to go to understand the requirements for long-range planning. In too many cases enlightenment will come only with enlightened replacements. Vested interests and perspectives from the past will make the transition slow and dangerous. Nevertheless, there are stirrings suggestive of a new approach.

There are other evidences of a shift in attitude and actions with regard to long-range planning.

For example, there is a growing awareness on the part of new city developers of the need to base their urban designs on systematic efforts to evolve in a coordinated manner both the physical and the social environment of those cities through their initial period of growth. As of 1967, Columbia, Maryland, was the outstanding case in point. Very early in Columbia's development, an interdisciplinary work group under my direction systematically sought to derive physical arrangements for an urban environment that would provide its citizens with more opportunities for personal and social growth and more access to them. The deliberations of this group, which included in its active membership the chief planner and the developer of Columbia, significantly influenced the basic characteristics of the city design.[4] It will take some fifteen years to complete Columbia's presently planned-for physical development. Hence, social planning sought to anticipate future technological and social trends in order that the way the city is developed in the near future does not close off options for desirable physical and social development in later years. The physical interrelationships of high- and low-density dwelling areas, automobile, bus, bike, and pedestrian traffic, educational, religious, and commercial buildings and recreational areas, together make more options available and more easily accessible for more people to live more fully. To the same end, new institutional arrangements have been established. For example, different religious denominations will share buildings and management and service resources. More integrated social, medical, and health services will operate, made possible in part by the physical arrangements developed to meet the social and material needs a civilized city should provide in the future. Of critical importance, new institutions are being developed that will help Columbia's citizens guide the evolution of Columbia in the years ahead so that it will continue to benefit from a long-range planning perspective toward the goals of individual and social growth for the city.

The federally sponsored Model Cities legislation is in-

---

[4] For a detailed description of this planning approach see Morton Hoppenfeld, "A Sketch of the Planning-Building Process for Columbia, Maryland," *Journal of the American Institute of Planners,* XXXIII, No. 5 (November 1967), 398.

tended to produce an analogous approach to the revitalization of old cities. In this program funds are conditional on the city undertaking integrated programs (in both the social and logical meanings of the word) to deal with its pressing urban problems. Given the nature of the problems, these programs must be long-range in perspective, and they must be evaluated and responsive to the implications of the evaluations. Since this is an upsetting approach for entrenched urban politics as these operate in the cities, states, and Congress, funds for the program are minuscule so far, compared to the need. To what extent the program will operate as intended remains to be seen, but the intention and the existence of some congressional support are the important signs from the standpoint of this chapter.

Completed in 1966 were four preliminary studies commissioned by the State of California from aerospace firms. These studies deliberately applied systems analysis and other long-range planning and design techniques to problems facing the state over the next two decades in transportation, crime and delinquency, sewage disposal, and information retrieval. That the motives for commissioning the studies were mixed and the quality of the products open to argument does not vitiate the point that this long-range approach to social problems had both appeal and potential utility. And certainly the rhetoric declaiming the goals of the poverty program and of the extended federal efforts in education espouses advanced planning and guidance over long time periods—even if the planning and guidance have been mostly far less than the goals require.

These growing preoccupations with planning in general, and long-range planning in particular, have encouraged the organization of specialized professional efforts to forecast alternate futures and to understand what must be done beforehand to mold the future. This is evidenced by the recent proliferation of professional groups and "invisible colleges" in universities, research centers, and foundations.[5] Significantly, these efforts often involve people and organizations that are influential in government and industry. Some of those actively involved are in government and industry, and some move into and out of government as their competences are needed and circumstances permit. Both the users and producers of these forecasting efforts are self-consciously seeking ways to usefully describe the characteristics of and preconditions for alternative futures in order that men may act in the present so as to make a preferred future more likely.

Along with this appreciation of the necessity for and increased feasibility of long-range planning there has begun to grow a sense that the changeover to long-range planning poses new and critical social and psychological issues. For example:

Democratic government as distinct from democratic society, implies confidence in every man's common sense, in his sufficiency for passing judgments on matters of general interest, and it requires the invigoration of every man's self-confidence in this respect. . . . If I compare my attitude to what it would have been two or three centuries ago, I find that I trust far less to the evidence of my senses, rely far more upon scientific authority, and am far more aware of my ignorance. A formidable expansion of human knowledge shows up the poverty of my own:

[5] Many of the footnotes specifically refer to such men, organizations, and products of study. So too does Ward Madden in the Foreword.

indeed this great age of science is, by way of corollary, an age of personal ignorance. . . . This psychological impact of science seems to me to work against sustaining this general confidence in one's judgment, which is basic to the conception of democracy.[6]

A major problem implicit in this situation is how to provide an educative environment that can teach one to recognize and acknowledge the basic change in the domains of citizen competence in a highly technological society, and yet not to abdicate a meaningful and applicable self-confidence. This will be especially hard to do, since many teachers will suffer from the erosion of self-confidence de Jouvenel describes. As such, they can hardly be adequate models or interpreters of the world they are trying to help educate others for. (We will return to this problem in the last chapter.)

The trend toward long-range planning seems evident then, and the problems the society faces and the growing power of planning-augmenting technologies strongly suggest that the trend will increase in pace and scale. With this background in mind we can now examine the critical bind we shall find ourselves in.

We have seen that we will be short of skilled human resources and of the time needed to do the things that need to be done. These scarcities alone, regardless of what other material and monetary limits there might be, mean that we will have to conserve our resources. We won't be able to do everything at once. We will have to assign social priorities and we will have to make sure that the resources allocated to them are used efficiently. We will have to act more deliber-

[6] Bertrand de Jouvenel, "The Political Consequences of the Rise of Science," *Bulletin of the Atomic Scientist* (December 1963), p. 8.

ately, more discriminatingly, more incisively, and more massively toward the social tasks to be done. We can't wait for the bigoted, the uneducated, the backward-looking, the vested interests to see the needs of the world of the future in their own good time: there isn't that kind of time left in which to cope with the complexities of this society before they become intractable—if they aren't already. So, to the extent we can, we will have to make it worthwhile for people to change. But who is this "we" that will do these things? The "we" consist of intellectually limited and emotionally crippled human beings, stumbling along on untested methodological crutches over a volcanic terrain of outmoded organizations. While we must and want to do long-range planning, we won't be able to do it well.

What about these people? For the most part, they represent those American values and experiences that produce in most of us large proportions of aggressiveness, guilt, sentimentality, status-seeking, manipulativeness, and defensiveness. Emotional needs such as these drive our scientists, technologists, government officials, and executives just as much as they do the ordinary citizen. Those who have succeeded in this society, particularly those who have attained positions of power, have usually done so by applying the drive these characteristics supply.

I am not asserting that leaders are *only* driven by personal needs that are corrupted or corruptible or that, because of these particular needs, nothing socially good can come from them or the organizations they are part of. But the point is that during the next couple of decades mixed motives will influence, as they always have, decisions about when to use for what ends whatever capabilities we have for doing long-range planning. Our society will not be run or responded to by people who are purely "objective," disinterested, logical, self-effacing souls, whatever their titles and tasks. If they were such, we very probably wouldn't know how to know it; and if they were such, they would very likely be so deviant in perspective and style that they would run afoul of the political or bureaucratic system long before they reached the point where they had the power to influence things very much.

Nor are planners, futurists, systems analysts, experts who write reports, and "think tanks," profit-making or not-for-profit, exempt from these weaknesses. Any one of the so-called professionally "disinterested" individuals or organizations would be hard put honestly to claim indifference to fame, fortune, status, the ear of the great, being "in" and thereby being "one up" on one's colleagues—or indifference as to where the next grant, contract, or endowment might come from. Some suffer from deeper gnawings of aggression, guilt, and all the other curses and drives of insecure men raised in an insecure society with little to define themselves by but transient ideas that almost never can be truly claimed as original. (And even when they are original, such is the noise and turmoil in the often savage marketplace of intellectual prestige and power seekers that one can never really prove possession. And such is the rate at which original ideas are signally modified by others that proof would be almost empty of significance.)

I stress this clay-footedness in leaders and their professional advisors because I am appalled at the extent to which expectations about the uses to which social and material technology will be put, and the results therefrom, tacitly assume pervasive good will, logic, and wisdom on the part of citizens and leaders. Instead we must be prepared for the fact that long-range planning will be done in a context of unprecedently powerful technology and typically weak men and institutions.

Combined with these personal needs and motives in politicians, technologists, planners, and policymakers are new institutional procedures, especially important here, that rely on the partial, i.e., incomplete, and partisan use of scientific knowledge.

Scientific arguments have become indispensable weapons in the struggle for power within the executive branch, and the scientific elites have become the providers of these weapons. Starting out as the disinterested purveyors of esoteric knowledge, the scientific elites end up by rationalizing and justifying the political interests by dint of their possession of esoteric knowledge. . . . This combination of esoteric knowledge and political power alters the function and character of scientific elites. They no longer merely advise on the basis of expert knowledge, but they are also the champions of policies promoted with unrivaled authority and frequently determined by virtue of it. In the eyes, both of the political authorities and the public at large, the scientific elite appears as the guardian of the *arcana imperii*, secret remedies for public ills.[7]

As I am using them, "partial" and "partisan" are not necessarily pejorative terms. They describe a persisting human circumstance. It is a circumstance that simply must be lived with from the standpoint of expeditious and feasible decision-making. The problem is how much can it be lived with from the standpoint of considered judgment and democratic par-

---

[7] Hans J. Morgenthau, "Modern Science and Political Power," *Columbia Law Review*, LXIV, No. 1386 (1964), 1401–1402.

ticipation. Thus, the question that preoccupies us here is whether customary institutions can cope adequately with the consequences of using partial and partisan scientific-technological knowledge to apply unprecedentedly powerful new technologies to the operation of an unprecedentedly complex society.

Scientific-technological knowledge will necessarily be incomplete, partial, when it is applied to social planning. Policies and decisions regarding technological applications will have to rest on plans conceived well ahead of the circumstances with which they are to deal. These plans, as well as the procedures for implementing them and for changing them as appropriate, will depend on projections and interpretations based on economic and social models of what society is and what it will be when the application is made. While these projections and interpretations will be based on substantially improving scientific knowledge about the character and dynamics of society, they will nevertheless be imperfect because there will not be at any time complete knowledge about man or his future.

What knowledge there is about the potentials and limits of new technologies and about the existing and anticipated state of society in which they will be used will be very useful knowledge indeed for political and economic decisions. Almost certainly, those who have it will try to control access to it so they can use it selectively to put their favored programs, evaluations, and expectations in the best light. For it will be large, labyrinthine, and politically skilled government agencies, closely allied with their aides, the nongovernmental technologists, who will facilitate most major technological developments and their applications to large social tasks defined and directed by an Administration. One way or the other, indeed in most ways, it will be the government that promotes and implements specific technologies for specific social ends, whether the end be space exploration, education, crime control, new-city building, or mental health. Only the government is obligated and organized to serve the public interest and only it will have the enormous coordinating resources and funds required to carry out such plans even when private enterprise is the government's chosen vehicle for implementing specific programs. Thus, the selection of new technologies for development, the rate of development, the scale of their application, and, very important, subsequent evaluations of their consequences will be increasingly governmentally determined, hence, subject to political considerations.

This being the situation, we can expect conventional political and bureaucratic procedures and motives for aggrandizement to persist. Executive offices and executive agencies, using what is advantageous to them from their not-for-profit and industrial "think tanks" and from their in-house suppliers of ideas and hardware, can be expected to operate formidable staffs that use information-manipulating technologies for the partisan promotion of their favored technology-based programs and for their protection once a political commitment has been made to them. For it will be by means of these methods, along with other social-engineering technologies, that arguments will be made and positions justified regarding the pros and cons of implementing specific social and physical technological innovations. These arguments will also include the issue of whether and how these "nonhardware" technologies should themselves be used to advance or retard some purpose. In other words, these social technologies will be used by one group to promote or disparage the proposed applications of social technologies by other groups, as well as to promote or disparage "hardware" applications.

. . . social science has and will have, to the extent that it explains and justifies our policy choices, not just a clinical and a rejective function, but a symbolic, a legitimatizing, and an ideological function. I argue, in other words, that in the sociological-anthropological perspective social scientists will have religious and political functions. We may protest in all honesty and with deep conviction that this is not our intent or desire, that we wish to function as scientists, pure and simple—but if old legitimacies crumble in the modern "crisis of authority," does not science itself raise a claim to legitimatize decision? I believe there is no denying that the social scientist will exercise much the same social role and function as the Roman temple priest who read the future from the entrails of oxen—though the social scientist reads it from graph, from report, from computer.[8]

Thus, the growth of big science, the increasingly causal relationship between science and technology, the social potency of the technologies, and the economic significance of big science will lead to more mutual political involvement both for the producers of technology and for its planner and politician users. As with other people, scientist-technologists become allied with the particular auspices in which they work or which their work serves. How many scientist-technologists working with NASA or its contractors speak against the manned moon program? During the debate a few years ago, who among the scientist-technologists associated with the Atomic Energy Commission or the Defense Department or

[8] Dwight Waldo, Comments on "Government, Politics and Administration," *Research for Public Policy* (Washington, D.C.: The Brookings Institution, 1961), p. 28.

their university or industrial contractors acknowledged the serious possibility of genetic damage to future generations from radioactive fallout from nuclear weapon-testing? How many Department of Agriculture scientists-technologists wondered out loud about the deleterious effects on the biosphere of the widespread use of pesticides? And who in the Surgeon General's Office acknowledged that they were tardy in undertaking studies of their effects on humans? Did the social and physical technologists working for the Office of Civil and Defense Mobilization ever publish a report questioning the social and physical feasibility of a national shelter system? In its initial stages, were there publicly expressed doubts from the offices of Project Head Start about its programmatic inadequacy based on what was already known from the very research that inspired the program? And have the Department of Labor's economists ever been other than sanguine publicly about the impact of automation on the work force?

Inevitably, under these circumstances of partial knowledge and political and organizational commitment, the arguments pro and con for the use of a particular technology and the "facts" and interpretations of the facts on which these arguments will be based will be partial, selective, in what they emphasize or exclude. In this way the arguments will be heavily partisan, depending for their emphasis on the intentions, values, and other circumstances that characterize the promoters or deprecators of a particular technology and its potential users. Because of the enormous complexity of the issues and of the authority and prestige of the sponsors of a particular approach, it will be difficult to determine the degree to which the argument is partial and partisan, or to determine the significance and sufficiency of the argument for the issue at hand. The mixture of exotic technological knowledge and politics (in both the producers and the users of the technology) will make it exceedingly difficult to document where technological definitions of "reality" leave off and political definitions of "reality" begin.

An example here is Operation Head Start where practically before the first summer's exercise was over the President and the OEO were declaring it a rampant success. Over a year later, and with no fanfare at all, evaluation indicated the success was far more limited and that its long-term success, as measured by the initial goal, was very doubtful if no major improvements were made in lower-school environments to back up the Head Start experience. This precondition for success was insisted on by the scientists who had done the research that inspired Head Start. But their concerns were overridden in the drive to get a politically attractive program under way fast on a large scale. Today, little has been done to match the action and political hurrah of the Head Start program with an appropriate follow-on program in the first grades—the evaluation has not been allowed to spoil the promise of quick success, of instant humanity, that made the initial commitment politically feasible.

The situation will become even harder to deal with when, as will often be the case, there is an interlocking of technological vested interests, the public interest, and private profit. Representative Wright Patman, chairman of the House Economic Progress Subcommittee of the Joint Economic Committee, gives an example:

It is essential, of course, that the tremendous technical know-how of our society be directed toward solving problems in this area of great social need [i.e., education]. There's danger, however, that many school systems and educational institutions may be committed for many years to unsuitable or inadequate teaching equipment and programs, simply because of the large investment required to produce and install any equipment and program, and to train teaching personnel to use them, will preclude reconsideration of choices once they are made.

Options for change must be held open. It would be tragic if control of curriculum and the content of courses were to pass by default into the hands of large corporate producers in the "hardware" or "software" end of the business. Teaching aids and devices should be developed to meet explicit educational objectives and needs, rather than to broaden markets for particular products.

In the years ahead, it should be a primary concern of public policy to safeguard this role while promoting the utmost improvement of productivity in our educational programs through the studied application of the new technology.[9]

But Representative Patman doesn't indicate how public policy will cope with the danger he foresees or implement the public policy role he recommends. For the trend seems to be to use public funds and political commitment to stimulate profit-making industries to develop, install, and maintain such equipment. Such interlocking of interests will make it very difficult to establish and implement means for setting the public interest clearly ahead of others.

Moreover, when the government mobilizes vast resources over the objections of significant political opposition, it takes on a very heavy momentum of commitment and very often this is transferred to subsequent Administrations (e.g., the space program and Vietnam). This will also be the case with practically any seriously mounted longer-range plan. It is very hard with our existing style of politics to admit mis-

---

[9] Wright Patman, "Automation, Technology, and Education," *The Quarterly*, XVIII, No. 3 (February 1967), 2–7.

takes, to shift gears openly and in an articulated manner, or to stop a misguided program.

Massive change demands massive commitments and hence no small element of rigidity. Unpredictable change demands flexibility. Change both massive and unpredictable makes inconsistent demands for rigidity on the one hand and flexibility on the other, and poses the most basic policy choice of all, the choice of what to regard as regulatable. . . . Such decisions may also be politically impossible to make in cultures which, like those of Western societies today, find the confession of impotence intolerable.[10]

Several aspects of this problem of coping with the partisan and partial use of scientific-technological knowledge are nicely represented in this excerpt from a *New York Times* editorial:

Supporters of Government subsidies for the supersonic passenger plane have continually stressed that it is needed to strengthen the nation's balance of payments. But a special report made for the Federal Aviation Agency and kept secret until now punctures this sales pitch. Far from helping to reduce the deficit in the balance of payments, the report by the Institute for Defense Analysis suggests that the SST may actually add to it. The report states that the gains from foreign sales of an American SST will be more than offset by a big increase in American tourist spending abroad as well as by a reduction in sales of subsonic American planes. The F.A.A. disputes this analysis. . . .[11]

Nevertheless, partial as the state of knowledge may be about the utility of a technology and partisan as the pro-

10 Sir Geoffrey Vickers, *The Art of Judgment* (New York: Basic Books, 1965), p. 81.
11 Editorial, "Supersonic Economics," *The New York Times*, May 21, 1967.

moters of particular technological applications may be, this knowledge will have to be used one way or the other to better the existing environment and to get ready for the future. And one way or another, good long-range planning must have continuing, candid evaluation of what is happening in the light of what was planned for, and it must be able to respond to it. Without such influential evaluation, the plan becomes mere rhetoric or, worse, it becomes counterproductive because those directing it are unable to discover if it is still oriented to its goals. But continuous evaluative feedback that is useful and is intended to be used is precisely what will be upsetting to most members of inherently self-protective organizations. In the nature of the world we are anticipating, things are likely to go wrong at least as often as they go right.

And here too are serious problems. For indications to date suggest that present means will be profoundly inadequate for: (1) getting technological information to potential countervailing or supporting groups in the form needed for them to play an appropriately sophisticated role in determining which technologies to apply or to continue to apply in the pursuit of social goals; (2) providing those groups with the means for fully understanding what the information might mean; and (3) for doing all this in time and through procedures which would allow them to influence policy-oriented deliberations in ways compatible with the implementation of longer-range plans.

We must now examine another weakness in our long-range planning abilities: our methods are untested and inadequate. Much of the knowledge we need, in order to understand man and society well enough to know what we want to plan for, is presently unavailable. It will take time to acquire. And much of the knowledge we need in order to know how to plan well is unavailable too. It can only be gained by studying the very processes and consequences of planning.

What's more, some of the needed knowledge can only be obtained from direct observation of people and from studies which require keeping records of individuals' behavior over many years. Studies aimed at improving these research methods and the dissemination of the findings from such research will conflict with some people's beliefs about the right to individual and group privacy. These beliefs will be changing under the impact of the changing social context described earlier. But, as described earlier, the rate and kind of change will vary in this area of belief and conduct as in others. There will continue to be confusion over the meaning and worth of various aspects of the conduct of privacy in our changing society, and over the proper balance between the public interest and the practices of privacy. Then too, some of those opposed to long-range planning will use the issue of privacy-invasion as a tactic for delaying the acquisition of knowledge needed to plan well. For many reasons, then, efforts to prevent "invasions of privacy" will from time to time slow the acquisition of knowledge needed for better long-range planning.

Related critical factors in the methodological area are emphasized in the following quotations from experts skilled both in theoretical and practical areas of planning, of "future thinking."

Since the material world is a system, any change in the given is bound to have numberless, often unpredictable, repercussions throughout the system; so even if the effect of the intervention is to bring under control the variable which is directly affected, the total system is likely to be less predictable than before, while all learned skills based on the former "given" are depreciated. Further, these interventions, and the further interventions to which their unpredicted results are bound to lead, are likely to be self-multiplying. The rate of change increases at an accelerating speed, without a corresponding acceleration in the rate at which further responses can be made; and this brings ever nearer the threshold beyond which control is lost.[12]

It is not at all clear that the [planning and programming] methods which have worked within the unitary managerial system of an industrial aerospace corporation can also be made to work within the pluralistic political system of local government. Sources of funding are very different. The distribution of authority is far more dispersed in the public arena. Goals of cities' populations are far more diverse and more frequently competing. And the fundamental epistemologies are extremely different.[13]

Let me put this another way. Our data and theory about the behavior of men and institutions are limited. They are, however, already great enough to be often useful when correctly applied. They will become more powerful as we do the social research described earlier. In the critically important task of predicting the future, our techniques are limited and untried: we have no proven methods or experts when it comes to long-range predictions. If we do have methods and experts, we won't know it until we are well along into the time period that we want to be able to plan for *now*.

[12] Sir Geoffrey Vickers, "Ecology, Planning, and the American Dream," in Leonard J. Duhl (ed.), *The Urban Condition* (New York: Basic Books, 1963), pp. 374–395.

[13] C. West Churchman and Melvin M. Webber, "Technology and Urban Management Project," Semi-annual Report to NASA, University of California in Berkeley, August 1966, pp. 10–11.

The result of this situation will be that we will not worry about whether the forecasts are really correct in the sense of forecasting a future perceived as "sitting out there waiting for us." Instead we will use forecasts as a means of bringing about, of engineering, changes intended to increase the likelihood of attaining a desired future from among plausible futures. To do this will require the ability to change men and institutions and to keep track of unprecedentedly large and complex social systems with their complex feedback, which gets us into the problem Sir Geoffrey referred to. While our capacity to change men and institutions is improving, it is not so great that the changes can be made easily or quickly. (Indeed, it may turn out that increasing knowledge about the nature of man will make it clear that such changes cannot be made both quickly and felicitously.) Since we lack the ability to make the changes needed at the pace and on the scale necessary to cope with the problems we foresee, or to make a world we want as quickly as we think we need it, we badly need data and theory to deal with the turmoil, the social disruptions, that are the likely consequences of our incapacity to change ourselves quickly and coherently. But the consequences of such turmoil are unpredictable—such upsets are "discontinuities" in the social system, shifting it into new arrangements, new stabilities. Our formal knowledge of the dynamics of social disruption is minuscule especially as regards the kind of society we have been talking about. In the absence of theory about the results of disruption, we can act to try to avoid disruption, but so acting is precisely one of the chief reasons why we must do long-range planning in the first place—which takes us full circle.

We will find ourselves then in the position of having social and physical technological knowledge that increasingly enables us to make profound changes in our world and ourselves, and we will find ourselves increasingly compelled to use that knowledge. At the same time that we do so, unanticipated consequences will loom larger. If they are bad, they are likely to be very bad indeed. Thus, during the time period we are looking at, our technological ability to change our world will exceed our ability to anticipate whether we are using it wisely. Of utmost importance, we will not know whether our plans are resulting in new political processes and social values that further democracy and personal growth in the spirit of the Judeo-Christian ethos. Not using our planning capability is, of course, no solution as such: it's simply a decision to do something else. We are almost certain to face disaster if we don't plan; we are almost certain to increase the likelihood of having a better world if we plan well. But we are also almost certain to be in deep trouble even with planning because our best plans will be developed and fostered by limited human beings picking and choosing among limited knowledge, very often ignorant of the extent of their own ignorance.

The usual response to this lesser-of-two-evils vision is to urge that new organizations be created in order to do things better and to educate so as to provide the leaders and citizens to utilize these institutions. Let us turn to these "solutions" to see what is involved in realizing them.

5

THE NATURAL RESISTANCES
TO ORGANIZATIONAL CHANGE

THERE ARE TWO KINDS of organizational change. They affect each other, but they also usually occur relatively independently (though the most efficacious situation often pertains when they occur in response to each other).

These are changes in the means for attaining the values and goals of the organization, and changes in the values and goals themselves within the organization as such and in its relations with its outside environment. Both kinds of changes will be necessary if we are to use long-range planning to help make a more felicitous world. While changes in operating methods are easier to accomplish than changes in values and goals (in the absence of organizational disasters, that is), both are very difficult to attain. Consider, for example, Rensis Likert's conclusions about the time needed to introduce participative management methods of the kind developed by him and his colleagues.

92

Field experiments conducted by the Institute for Social Research in several companies indicate that at least three or four years are likely to be necessary to develop and test the application of the newer theory [of participative management] in a particular company. In companies with more than two or three hundred employees, an additional five years or more may be required to shift the organization to a full-scale application of the newer theory. In large corporations, even more time will be necessary.

Neither the testing of the theory nor the shifting of an organization to a full-scale application of the theory can be hurried. Haste is self-defeating because of the anxieties and stresses it creates. There is no substitute for ample time to enable the members of an organization to reach the level of skillful and easy, habitual use of the new leadership and membership principles and methods required for an application of the newer theory.

The decisions a company makes today, consequently, with regard to the extent it uses social science research and experimentally tests new theories, principles, and practices will exert a major influence on the character and effectiveness of its management system a decade hence.[1]

One source of this resistance to change derives from the interdependence and interlockedness of organizations. Another source is what might not unreasonably be called neurologically based resistance to relearning, once one has learned successful behavior. At the psychological level, there is the strong disinclination to jeopardize a satisfying self-image, based on that success, that sustains those who would have to take the risks to self and organization inherent in changing both. Some critical internal dynamics of this circumstance merit explication, especially when the giver of the description

[1] Rensis Likert, *New Patterns of Management* (New York: McGraw-Hill Book Company, Inc., 1961), pp. 247–248.

is both an executive in a major corporation and a careful student of the processes of executive behavior.

It seems that the leaders of business, labor, and government . . . have today many more similarities in their viewpoints than differences. The present leaders naturally attempt to use the past to present the image of the future, conserving the values and attitudes which have made present institutions and organizations successful. They search for ways in which the present technological changes can be viewed as normal evolution. The problem, as seen through the eyes of our leaders, is to find agencies for our present imbalances, to provide stimulus to the already existent institutions, and to take care to provide the balance between change and stability—in such a way that our basic economic and political systems suffer minimum change. Their approach in general is to seek our adjustments, to intensify or weaken various operative forces, and to make present institutional formats work with minimum change. This is the conservative view and it guarantees that the future will preserve to the maximum extent the shape of those ideas which guaranteed success in the past.[2]

This situation is no casual accident easily rectifiable by "good will" and "good intentions." It arises from bedrock social and psychological processes that are most difficult to change quickly or broadly. A political scientist and specialist on institutional processes reaches the following conclusion:

There is not much point, then, in musing about how nice it would be if our corporate managers underwent more instruction in moral philosophy or modern sociology. The simple fact is that they are busy men, on the way up during most of their formative years, and the exigencies of the climb compel them to think of them-

[2] Charles R. DeCarlo, "Perspectives on Technology," in Eli Ginzberg (ed.), *Technology and Social Change* (New York: Columbia University Press, 1964), pp. 21–22.

selves rather than for themselves. This is an inevitable consequence of opening careers to the talented, of breaking down the
barriers that once prevented men of inauspicious backgrounds
from rising to the top.[3]

And a psychiatrist who, as a member of the public health
service, has dedicated most of his professional life to trying
to introduce the preconditions for long-range planning into
the top levels of federal executive agencies makes this observation:

The introduction of a planning and forecasting mechanism necessarily raises a tremendous amount of tension and anxiety in
the staff primarily because the setting of new and different long-
range goals automatically raises questions about current proceedings. . . . This problem of inertia, of the unwillingness to
give up familiar and functional patterns of behavior in favor of
new ones will be encountered at all levels of an organization.
. . . Planning and forecasting mechanisms often are in direct
competition with the power structure that is based primarily on
the pyramidal model of organizational structure.[4]

These organizational and personal resistances to change
are reinforced by the complexity of our society: it is easy for
an organization to so obscure its actions and operating environment that it is hard to find out what's really happening
and, hence, what changes ought to be demanded. In his
book, *The Image,* the historian Daniel Boorstin describes the
rise and consequences of what he calls the "pseudo-event,"

[3] Andrew Hacker, "The Making of a (Corporation) President,"
The New York Times Magazine (April 2, 1967), pp. 26–27 ff.
[4] Leonard J. Duhl, "Creation of Forecasting and Planning Mechanisms," Working Papers of the Commission on the Year 2,000 of
the American Academy of Arts and Sciences, Vol. III, 1966 (limited
circulation).

the planned, planted, or incited event, the non-natural event. With regard to the role of the reporter he says,

If he wishes to keep his news channels open he must accumulate a vocabulary and develop a style to conceal his sources and obscure the relation of a supposed event or statement to the underlying facts of life, at the same time seeming to offer hard facts. Much of his stock in trade is his own and other people's speculation about the reality of what he reports. He lives in a penumbra between fact and fantasy. He helps create that very obscurity without which the supposed illumination of his reports would be unnecessary. A deft administrator these days must have similar skills. He must master "the technique of denying the truth without actually lying." . . . Pseudo-events thrive on our honest desire to be informed, to have "all the facts," and even to have more facts than there really are. . . . Our "free market place of ideas" is a place where people are confronted by competing pseudo-events and are allowed to judge among them. When we speak of "informing" the people this is what we really mean.[5]

Thus, what gets emphasized, what gets defined as reality, as important, often has little to do with what needs to be done and what changes need to be made to do it. A revealing example is worth introducing here. The Report of the National Commission on Technology, Automation, and Economic Progress was widely hailed for its imaginative and relatively outspoken recommendations about what to do to meet the potential problems of employment and unemployment produced by automation over the next decade. But

It is one thing to bell the cat by making the recommendations. It is quite another thing to make those profound institutional

[5] Daniel J. Boorstin, *The Image* (New York: Harper and Row, 1961), pp. 34–35.

changes that pervade all of society, in order to carry through those recommendations. It's still another thing—the most difficult thing of all—to make these changes fast.

This institutional change process, and indeed the political and the value change process that goes with it, become all the more central if we take the report seriously regarding the need to provide economic and other resources quickly in order to deal with the consequences of increased productivity and technological change over the next decade. . . . This means then that these changes must happen rapidly if they are to be effective during the next decade, and they have to occur pervasively. What's more in many cases we will have to do much research quickly regarding motivation, learning, social mobility, etc., before we will have the knowledge needed to act. Yet there is nothing in the report regarding this timing problem, not even a candid acknowledgement.[6]

Without massive institutional change the recommendations of the Commission will remain chiefly an admirable gesture. But to know this a reader would have to appreciate how difficult such change is to accomplish and why it would need to be accomplished, considerations that are not likely to be foremost in most people's minds, especially when they are dazzled by the aura of comprehensiveness such a report carries, induced by the pseudo-eventish prestige of a presidential commission comprised of national leaders.

Given the difficulties of making massive institutional changes fast enough, what are the implications for the conduct of long-range planning? In the last chapter I mentioned some of the human and methodological weaknesses characterizing those in government (and in its extended,

[6] Remarks of Donald N. Michael in "The Report of the President's Commission on Automation—A Critique," *Public Affairs Conference Report*, No. 4 (New York: National Industrial Conference Board, Inc., 1966), p. 36.

nongovernmental "staff" of contractors and advisors) who will have the task of planning wisely. Traditionally we have expected the general public to act as the ultimate guardian of its interests by understanding its interests and protecting them through its elected representatives and lobbies. This traditional belief is more myth than fact, of course. Angus Campbell and his collaborators state, on the basis of thorough research, that the general electorate is

almost completely unable to judge the rationality of government actions; knowing little of particular policies and what has led to them, the mass electorate is not able to appraise either its goals or the appropriateness of the means chosen to serve these goals. . . . However great the potential ability of the public to enforce a set of concrete policy demands at the polls, it is clear that this power is seldom used in American politics.[7]

Political sophisticates and cynics have assumed this long before the behavioral science data verified it. In fact, the system depends on the opinion-makers, the educated and politically active *fraction* of the population, and on their organized groups to play the roles of critic, supporter, and threat to power structures in and out of government. The question I am raising here is whether this fraction will be able to stay in touch with, find out about, and act on the kind of knowledge and information that will increasingly become the basis for arguing for one social policy rather than another and for implementing and evaluating it. For knowledge and the procedures for manipulating and interpreting knowledge will become increasingly esoteric as we expand the use of systems

[7] Angus Campbell, Philip E. Converse, Warren E. Miller, Donald E. Stokes, *The American Voter* (New York: John Wiley & Sons, Inc., 1960), pp. 543, 545.

analysis, simulated models of physical and social processes, and the like to provide and assess the information needed for decision-making, policy-planning, or political maneuvering. If the politically active layman is to bring his customary leverage to bear pro or con a proposed plan or to express his satisfaction with the alleged evaluation of how and where the plan is going, he needs to be able to do at least the following:

He will have to think in terms of many variables, probabilistically related, circularly reacting upon one another as cause and effect, and doing so in an evolution of interactions that take place over long time periods, periods well beyond the perspectives familiar to him. Few people think these ways today even among the politically active and "educated" minority of the population.

To apply common sense to what is visible on the surface is to be almost always wrong; it produces about as good an idea of how the world goes round as that afforded by the Ptolemaic system. A true grasp of even the simplest transaction requires special knowledge and the ability to use abstractions which, like the Copernican system, are at odds with common-sense impressions. Without this kind of knowledge, it is difficult to know what to think about even such prominent matters as the United Nations financing problem, or the bombing of North Vietnam, or the farm program, or the federal budget—which is one reason that most people don't know what they think about these questions. The simple fact is that the stuff of public life eludes the grasp of the ordinary man. Events have become professionalized.[8]

He will have to discover what overt and covert goals a plan is to serve, what variety of assumptions for attaining the

[8] Joseph Kraft, "Politics of the Washington Press Corps," *Harper's Magazine* (June 1965), pp. 101–102.

goals have been explored, and what computer-programming constraints were placed on the simulation models used for assessing the merits of the alternative approaches. It is not only the data that determine the relative merits, the comparative costs and benefits of alternative approaches to attaining a planned-for goal. It is the model the data are applied to and the constraints set on the way the data are manipulated in the model that also determine the outcomes. This is true whether we are trying to find out if it is feasible to get a man on the moon by a certain time in a certain way; or if one national military strategy rather than another gives more "bang for a buck"; or what is to be expected of particular approaches to mass transit or water purification or a computer-assisted, national, basic education scheme. But as we have seen, getting such information will not be easy because such information is politically valuable. And the more complex the problem, the harder it is to know whether one has gotten the information.

He will have to get at and decide the above before an Administration or an agency is committed and the program initiated. Even today this is exceedingly difficult to do. One of the most frustrating and least successful activities today is trying to find out enough in time and in detail to propose an alternative program before the government program becomes a *fait accompli* with so many vested interests established and so many operational wheels set in motion that it can't be stopped. Tom Wicker of *The New York Times* describes one result of this situation:

Vietnam and the racial question are the most dramatic and emotional issues in modern American life. They cause profound reactions among those concerned, and hone questions of personal responsibility to a far sharper point than most political or social situations. Therefore, the intellectuals anguished at the war and the Negroes who have all but abandoned hope for white recognition of their humanity, have only been forced more quickly than most others to the knowledge that in the vast impersonality of 20th Century society and government, it has become almost impossible for individuals to affect the grinding course of things.

That is the malaise beyond dissent—the fear that dissent does not matter any more; that only action counts; but that no one really knows what action to take. More and more, 20th Century man crouches like an old woman on her stoop, pointing her rusty shotgun at the oncoming expressway, knowing all the time that in the end the bulldozers will go through.[9]

Thus, the means for democratic participation in the governance of tomorrow's society are not at all clear. It will be necessary to get public support for long-range programs, to transform customary perspectives into those appropriate for the needed programs, and to do so in the short time and on the large scale required. Deeper understanding of the nature of public opinion, better methods for collecting information about the state of society in general and public opinion in particular, and more refined models for using public-opinion feedback to further influence public opinion will increase our ability to "engineer" this consent. The use of such techniques seems to be necessary in view of the desperate need to deal with the precarious social conditions described earlier. But there will also be the looming probability that the manipulation of consent will not be used solely in a disinterested manner—even if "disinterest" were to be deemed an ethical basis

[9] Tom Wicker, "The Malaise Beyond Dissent," *The New York Times,* March 12, 1967, p. E13.

for such manipulations. Those with a policy to sell or a program to maintain will have a vested interest in initiating it and continuing it. As C. R. Bowen put it,

We must make certain the magnitude of the achievements we will surely witness will not silence our citizens into an awed and amazed compliance with the status quo. As we are better able to organize men and machines for productive purposes, there will be a great temptation to apply breakthroughs in the life and social sciences to make of the citizen a compliant automaton. Never since the American Revolution has dissent and the questioning of orthodoxy been more important to the continued life of the Republic. In a period of such complexity and specialization it is almost inevitable that the vast majority of dissent will be primarily irrelevant or thoroughly crackpot. But there lives no genius who can discern the tiny fraction which harbors the creative insight necessary to continue reshaping our society and prevent it from becoming frozen or clumsy in adapting to the changes being generated so rapidly.[10]

This means that we will need to invent appropriate institutions to provide checks and balances for such a world as we have been envisioning. For example, I have been suggesting that equal time on TV to rebut the opposition will not be enough. The "outs" will also need full access to the data, programs, and computer facilities of an Administration so that its public assertions about what its planners, evaluators, and programmers tell it can be checked along with the assumptions and the conclusions based on them. Another check and balance could be a requirement that the Administration expose the behavioral models on which it bases its

[10] Charles R. Bowen, "Automation: The Paradoxes of Abundance," in William W. Brickman and Stanley Lehrer (eds.), *Automation, Education and Human Values* (New York: School and Society Books, 1966), p. 82.

techniques for influencing various publics, along with the data used to operate them. Or, as with a court-appointed lawyer, the "outs" might be guaranteed access to first-rate theory applicable for "engineering consent," along with skilled practitioners and all the social data they need to apply their chosen strategy for persuading a constituency. Obviously these situations are not just around the corner but they do suggest that providing the "outs" with the information needed to participate in choosing among plans and in influencing their ongoing revision is going to take more than good will to accomplish.

What's more, in addition to inventing these new social institutions we will need to invent *other* institutions that will facilitate the initiation of such inventions. For, as we have seen, it is very unlikely that the membership of a secure organization is voluntarily going to subject itself to the disruption of perspective, status, and operations that radical new approaches would require.

Nor does it particularly help to argue that the long-range plan is no good if there is opposition to it. There is bound to be opposition to any worthy plan somewhere along the line by some significant portion of the population: no consent-engineering techniques of the next few decades will eliminate all significant opposition. Resort to the political process of "reconciling differences" will not solve the problem either. As presently practiced, it is one of the chief reasons we get so few well-articulated plans, so little significant evaluation, and so little done when it needs to be done. The resultant compromises usually mean the plan, such as it is, is gerry-rigged. Careful evaluation of the implemented "plan" is bound to reveal its inadequacies. Hence the evaluation is not done and, thereby, the compromisers are protected. Since resistance to social planning in any given case comes in part from those who have a vested interest in the way things are, part of the compromise usually involves slowing down the rate or scale on which things are changed.

The chances are not good—not impossible but not really good—that the socially conscious, socially active youth of this generation are going to radically make over the policy-planning and policy-implementing complex of interlocking national organizations during the next couple of decades or so. Institutional change is so difficult and the numbers of social activists are so few to do the job. Of course, there will be circumstances wherein their skills and commitment will produce important local changes because individuals can more easily effect substantial local changes—which changes, incidentally, require very unlikely concatenations of circumstances in order to become more broadly implemented. But after I allow for the erosion that making a living and raising a family produce on devotion to radical social action, and after I discount the transient motivation of youthful rebellion per se, and, very important, after I subtract the many young social activists who will in later years find rewarding outlets for their concerns in activities in other than the planning, policy, and decision-making levels of large organizations, I don't anticipate that there will be very many left to take on formidably organized and entrenched interlocked institutions of government, industry, and allied non-profit apologists. As protesters and leaders of protests, as the vanguard of liberal politics, youth will doubtless influence the directions of the society from time to time—as it has already done—but the consequences of protest and the occasions for it, as well as the occasions for decisive political action, are indeterminate.

This indeterminacy means that such actions are unlikely to produce organizational and especially interorganizational restructuring both rapidly and coherently.

What basically lies behind these considerations is the completely unworked-through problem of whether a built-in potential for the disruption of long-range plans by vigorous and competent or simply noisy and perhaps violent oppositions is compatible with long-range planning. If it is not, then it looks like we lose the better world we want either way: by not carrying through on long-range plans or by preventing effective popular participation in altering their substance and direction.

✻ 6 ✻

SOME CHALLENGES
FOR EDUCATORS

THE PRECEDING CHAPTERS argue that, on the one hand, we face enormously complex issues, problems, and opportunities, and we will have to use unprecedentedly powerful means for responding to them, especially an improving capability to do long-range planning. On the other hand, we have seen that our ability to plan and to implement those plans will continue to be seriously limited by methodological, institutional, and human weaknesses. Consequently, we will live in a period of tremendous turmoil. This circumstance in turn will require still greater efforts at long-range planning and institutional change. The question explored in this chapter therefore is what, if anything, could be done through the processes of education to provide a generation of leaders and citizens better able to cope with such a tumultuous world.

Let me be clear at the outset: I am not undertaking to make recommendations on how to overcome the ornately interlinked pattern of weaknesses in our educational system and in the other institutions which it serves and by which it is molded. I hope I've made it clear that I don't believe we know enough about the nature of our society to conjure up such a set of recommendations, and one of the things we know least about is how to go about implementing any such set of recommendations as rapidly as we would need them realized in the light of what we face. I want to deal instead with only one aspect of the situation: an approach to educating a special cadre of intellectually and emotionally highly skilled people who thereby will possess necessary if not sufficent resources to apply more wisely what we know to the long-range planning of our society. We deal with this educative task relatively informally and fortuitously now. I believe the situation requires that we consider carefully doing so much more deliberately than we have. But even if it were agreed that everybody ought to be educated for the skills herein recommended, not everybody can be—indeed at this time most can't be—given the special resources needed and especially given the kind of teachers and the kind of attitude toward them required. I am dealing in this chapter, then, with a very special educative environment, not with a general scheme for society as a whole, and hence with a special set of value issues associated with such a selective approach.

I will begin with the question of what emotional and intellectual skills beyond those presently provided are needed by those who at whatever level in whatever organization would lead wisely—planners and policymakers, the "politicians" of tomorrow, the teachers and guides. I am assuming, too, that these skills must be cultivated from very early childhood to be truly the quality of the man; I doubt that they can be more than "laid on" when exposure first comes at, say, high school or college. To be sure, there are those who see the light suddenly at whatever age, but we cannot count on these to be sufficient for our needs.

We must put vastly more emphasis on educating for certain intellectual abilities. We must educate people to have long-range perspectives, to think in terms of many variables related to each other as probabilities rather than certainties and related as both cause and effect of each other. We must educate for logical skill in recognizing and working through the ethically and morally tortuous dilemmas implicit in the assignment of social priorities and in the risks involved in seeking to attain them. This logical skill must be complemented by deep familiarity with the history of ideas and of comparative ethics, since the recognition and resolution of ethical issues is as much a matter of extrarational factors—historical accident and traditional values—as of purely rational assessments. We must educate so people can cope efficiently, imaginatively, and perceptively with information overload.

There are exhilarating educational changes under way that move partially in this direction. But they are not widespread, and they will not become widespread quickly, if only because present educational institutions are staffed largely by people educated toward the past, and many more such are still being produced, still being introduced into the system. Hence, we have far too few teachers able to teach these things because they are not cognitively sophisticated in these ways themselves. Computer-assisted instruction will doubtless be of great help over the long run, but it will only be over the long run.

In fact, the principal obstacles to computer-assisted instruction are not technological but pedagogical: how to devise ways of individualizing instruction and of designing a curriculum that are suited to individuals instead of groups. Certain obvious steps that take account of different rates of learning can be made with little difficulty; these are the main things that have been done so far. We have still, however, cut only a narrow path into a rich jungle of possibilities. We do not have any really clear scientific idea of the extent to which instruction can be individualized. It will probably be some time before a discipline of such matters begins to operate at anything like an appropriately deep conceptual level.[1]

When that time comes, economically supportable computer installations will have to be arranged for. We are not near this happy day in either sense at this point, though there are exciting pilot researches and applications that indicate we are getting closer.

With regard to the education of the feelings, the self, the emotions: we must educate for empathy, compassion, trust, nonexploitiveness, nonmanipulativeness, for self-growth and self-esteem, for tolerance of ambiguity, for acknowledgment of error, for patience, for suffering.

In the first place, those social-aid roles, the roles that are meaningful because they relate a person to a person, require such capabilities. Up until now, we have tended to treat the personal relationship in social-service support roles in that peculiar manner called "professional"—which assumes apparently that the service will be weakened if the practitioner becomes "personally involved" with the client. Such a viewpoint has served several purposes. It has made it easier for

---

[1] Patrick Suppes, "The Uses of Computers in Education," *Scientific American*, CCXV, No. 3 (September 1966), 208.

the professionals to have things convenient for them even if at the expense of the people they were supposed to serve. For example, studies of hospital procedures have made it amply clear that hospitals are generally set up for the convenience of the doctors and nurses rather than for the patients. Other studies document the same situation throughout the supporting services—including multiversities and schools in general. Remaining personally uninvolved has made it easier for the middle-class professional to avoid the personal anxiety and discomfort which could arise from any real contact with or understanding of his poor and dispossessed clients or students or patients. And in a social-service situation where there was too little money and too few personnel, it made for bureaucratic if not human "efficiency."

In tomorrow's world, with versatile technologies and with many more people unneeded in those blue collar, white collar, and service areas where machines can do the job as well, such an uninvolved "professional" attitude will be far less necessary. Indeed, often it will be destructive of both those who can feelingly and trustingly share of themselves and those who can respond to this sharing.

The other reason for deliberately undertaking this kind of education is that those who will have the tasks of planning and leading must have a far deeper feel for and understanding of themselves as selves and as a part of other persons, other selves, than they usually do today. Without such understanding, and the strength that comes with it, they will too easily succumb to pressures to engineer people rather than to encourage their self-discovery—and they will themselves be engineered in the process. Without this strength and understanding it will be too easy to succumb to what I have called "petite Eichmannism"—letting someone else worry about the ethical implications of what one is doing on the job. For as organizational arrangements, through which decisions are made and policies are carried out, become ever more interlocked, and as those decisions and policies become ever more complex, the incentives to overlook, to deny to oneself what one ought to be morally bound to examine will become great indeed. Without such educated, sensitized, emotional resources, leaders will continue to be too rigid, too defensive, too remote from themselves and thereby from others to have the flexible and bold state of mind that will be needed to cope humanely and imaginatively with plans and turmoil, order and disorder. It will take special efforts indeed to enlarge the emotional underpinning of those who recruit themselves to use the social technologies needed to run a complex society. But without such emotional resources to draw on, the Judeo-Christian tradition may be lost through the unfeeling overuse—or underuse—of rationalized means for producing aggregate solutions to mass problems.

Having seen what the educative environment—whatever its form—ought to produce in those experiencing it, we now need to appreciate some circumstances that drastically circumscribe what we can expect to accomplish now and in the middle future by way of producing this environment generally throughout the nation.

In the first place, in large part, those now growing into adulthood cannot be expected to be much more intellectually skilled, more compassionate, more in touch, than most of the "educated" generation that preceded them. This generation's education, by and large, has not been much different from that provided in the past. Some curriculum content and some teaching skills have improved substantially (for the relatively few exposed to them), but most teachers, school administrators, legislators, and parents are still driven by the same motives and living with essentially the same perspectives vis-à-vis the world's needs and the ways to meet them as their immediate predecessors. This condition of relative stasis is a consequence of the dependency of a public school system on the standards of the society for which it is educating new members. This is especially so since most of the leverage in the society has been associated with money, which means the "best" education has been popularly assumed to be that which the suburbanite affords his children. And

the child of suburbia is likely to be a materialist and somewhat of a hypocrite. He tends to be a striver in school, a conformist, and above all a believer in being "nice," polite, clean and tidy. He divides Humanity into the black and the white, the Jew and the Christian, the rich and the poor, the "smart" and the "dumb." He is often conspicuously self-centered. In all these respects, the suburban child patterns his attitudes after those of his parents.[2]

But, while schools have been turning out mostly the conventional suburban or slum products of education, the world, as we have seen, is getting much more complex. The upshot may well be that the majority of the new generation of adults and those new ones to come for several years yet will be more out of touch with their world than was, say, the correspondingly educated generation of an earlier day.

[2] Alice Milt and Edwin Kiester, Jr., "The Short-Changed Children," *The New York Times Magazine*, April 16, 1967, pp. 99 ff.

The British industrialist and cybernation expert, Sir Leon Bagrit, puts the difficulty this way in speaking of his own country and its leadership requirements for tomorrow's world:

Educationally, the task is a formidable one. We have at one and the same time to breed the type of administrator with an interest not only in the humanities—in philosophy, literature, economics, politics, in history or in the classics, but with some understanding of science, its history and philosophy, and of the direction in which science is moving . . .

Even if by some miracle the system I am proposing were instituted virtually here and now, it would take us something like ten years before the first of its products were available. In this highly critical next ten years we have somehow to make do with the leaders we have already got. It is interesting to wonder whether, in this respect anyway, we in this country are better off or worse off than other advanced nations? What assessment does one make of our existing stock leaders, the men already formed and educated and established . . . ? I myself think that we are rather inadequately provided.[3]

Sir Leon believes that England has more time to prepare than we, being behind us in the use of many technological resources. If he were speaking of the United States, and if he were not speaking in his understated style, what could he say about the crises *we* face? For if the new generation of relatively unaware adults is added to the older ones, there is a very large constituency to be convinced that radical changes are necessary fast to make education even *eventually* responsive to this coming world. Echoing Sir Leon, what I am saying is that it's too late now to do much about the capabilities

[3] Leon Bagrit, *The Age of Automation* (New York: New American Library, 1965), pp. 71, 73.

of today's leaders and citizens or even of most of those of tomorrow. But if we don't get started today, we won't have done enough to produce adequate citizens for the *day after* tomorrow—those who will have to cope somehow with the accumulated wonders and enormities that will grow from today's and tomorrow's problems and opportunities.

In the second place, educational institutions as much as, indeed often more than, many other institutions suffer from the inhibitions and resistances to change discussed in the previous chapter. Changes in teaching substance and teaching personalities depend on changes in the personalities and in the institutions that support and direct education. These organizations are large, varied, and ornately interlocked politically, economically, ideologically, and professionally. And for the most part, the organizations and the people who comprise them are products of a successful past. Most of today's teachers and educational administrators were themselves educated, and are still being educated, on the basis of social perspectives that are insensitive to the cognitive and emotional requirements emphasized here. Most primary and secondary schoolteachers—and this is the level, if not earlier, where these things have to be taught—come from backgrounds more at ease with a conservative view of life, suspicious of the strange, the innovative, the spontaneous, comfortable with the requirements, certainties, rewards, and the moral assurances of the Protestant ethic. Hence, there is no reason to suppose that, short of disaster, major, widespread changes are likely to be the lot of education in general over the next decades at least. There will be many small changes, in many places, and a few large changes in a few places, but not many large changes in enough places ade-

quate to cope with the societal snarls anticipated herein.
What's more, radical changes in the educational system itself could not occur unless there were complementary radical
institutional changes throughout the social system. That is,
radical changes in the educational system alone will be necessary, but will not in themselves be sufficient to deal with
the kinds of emotional, intellectual, and institutional problems outlined herein.

One reason we are in such short supply of such intellectually skilled people today and so tardy in preparing more of
them for tomorrow is that we have had and have so few with
such skills who have successfully insisted that there be the
opportunity to learn them. Our institutions have generally
evolved in a social environment which thrived (in some
senses) on preoccupation with the present and a more or less
laissez-faire style of institutional entrepreneurship. The tight
net of temporal and functional interdependence requiring the
cognitive skills stressed here is much newer than the prevail-
ing institutional forms. Not needing these skills for institutional growth in the past, few were willing to allocate resources to provide them on the large scale now required.

Certainly we do not educate systematically and widely to
cultivate the emotional and interpersonal characteristics described here. We hardly do so at all. Some fortunate few have
learned them "on their own" from either a great human or
situational teacher. But generally speaking, the large majority
of those in the generations now moving into adulthood are
not only inadequately educated, they are maleducated in
these areas.

Probably necessary conditions for learning these characteristics are teachers who possess them and a society that re-

wards them. But since our society has not signally rewarded these personal characteristics in comparison with the more conventional emotional inadequacies that have facilitated getting to the top, it is not surprising that we now have few teachers who possess them. In past times of slower change the model of the teacher as an essentially neutral device, facilitating the transformation of information about the world into student knowledge and behavior, was the appropriate one. The teacher's task was chiefly to conserve the past, to present it to the next generation in order that the past would be present in the future behavior, attitudes, styles of the next generation of adults. This made sense when the future was expected to be and indeed was intended to be like the present—which was like the past. This conserving function made so much sense that other institutions surrounded teachers with all sorts of sanctions so that their personal beliefs and behaviors would conform or appear to conform with the tradition. In this way, possibly "deviant" behavior was prevented from becoming a model from which the next generation might learn, though fortunately there were exceptions to this pattern. In most cases, this is still true and the teacher or administrator who does not conform to the conventional wisdom in statement and behavior is seen by many parents, legislators, educational administrators, and teachers as dangerous or at least unprofessional. Indeed, in most conventional school situations mutual fear of reprisal among students, teachers, and administration is a basic emotional reality. Such a situation hardly encourages the demonstration or learning of trust and compassion. Of course, there have always been exceptions, too, to this destructive emotional reality and there are more exceptions today. But over all the rate of change is slow, the opportunities to try few, and courage or charisma to lead lacking.

Institutional interlocking and the dominant perspectives of the society—including those of most of its new adults—suggest another reason why we have not educated for the kinds of thinking and feeling emphasized here, why it will be very hard to do so on a very wide scale in the years just ahead. Such education inevitably will produce the desire and capacity for radical questioning of the nature and purposes of self and society with all the threats this implies for the established ways of valuing and doing.

It is from among the brightest young people, who have the will to know themselves as well as others as selves, that most of the radical questioning comes today. They question not only by the ways they live, by the new social arrangements they are experimenting with, but by the values they put to test in the real world by actively protesting some aspects of it, intensely engaging in other aspects, and by withdrawing from still others. Whatever kinds of persons and circumstances they needed to produce in them this radical questioning state of mind and conduct will be needed too for many more. But perhaps in different forms and content, for it isn't clear that what most of these youth are finding is what's needed to run a huge society with its powerful technologies and necessary long-range plans. Maybe what most of them have found so far is something of what is needed as a counterpoise or alternative to be lived and cherished in the interstices of the big society. The point here is that we have ample evidence that radical questioning in thought and action is upsetting and anxiety-provoking, sometimes fury-provoking. As such, much as radical questioning is a necessary concomitant

of intellectual and emotional education for living fully in tomorrow, we won't get such education as the mode in anything like today's public educational institutions with their
personal and societal vested interests.

It seems to me, then, that the most we can do in the immediate future is to try deliberately to develop the needed
capabilities in the relatively few people accessible to the rare
appropriate educative environment and hope that the products of such education will be at the right place at the right
time to make the right difference in the actions that affect our
society for better or worse. Indeed, the "right place" may very
well be in a "societal interstice" where there may develop or
be preserved a different standard and life style. Thereby, at
some later, more propitious time this enclave or subculture
could serve as model for many other people as our larger society struggles to find its confused and dangerous way.

It is entirely possible for a comparatively few teachers,
administrators, and students to work together along the lines
I suggest below. Indeed, there always have been a few such.
That is why I argue that the implications of this specific kind
of effort ought to be seriously examined *independently* of the
usual recommendations for massive and drastic changes in
the processes and environment of education—recommendations for massive changes in the education role of industries,
unions, cities *as* cities, and so on. Such massive changes have
to come about if society is ever to be able to do long-range
planning truly well and, thereby, to consistently increase its
chances of reducing its problems and embracing its opportunities. But these are the kinds of multi-institutional changes
that we don't know how to accomplish quickly. Deliberately
attempted, these changes themselves would have to be based
on long-range planning and all that we have seen this implies.

Accidentally or deliberately, such changes might also come about as the result of the fluid conditions for reorganization that the occasion of social or physical disaster provides. I do expect to see, in the years ahead, particular corporations, affiliations, and communities choose to experiment with and contribute to radical educative transformations by becoming new types of educative environments for their members. And in these environments I expect to see some teachers of the kind I am recommending herein. But I am not proposing what I recommend here as a realistic target for education *in general* in the years immediately ahead. For all the reasons set out in the earlier chapters, I don't believe a general transformation could come about in any realistic way in the time period we're concerned with. In particular, there are the difficulties produced by the projection of past political motives and values into the future, the resistances of institutions to change, and our still fledgling capabilities for implementing what some people and institutions do think they know and want.

What I urge seems both possible on a limited scale and necessary, given the circumstances of the present and the anticipated character of the future; i.e., some teachers, their administrators, the parents of their students—and the students as much as the teachers—must recognize that preparing for tomorrow requires that the teacher teach *styles* of life as much or more than the "facts" of life. The teacher will have to *be* the world in order to teach about it.[4]

---

[4] By "teacher" I include other persons and circumstances as well as those experienced in the "school" setting. However, because children and youth will be spending more time being educated, and because education, whatever its place and content, will have increasing importance, thus endowing educators with increasing status, formally designated "teachers" will be especially important.

For these teachers the neutral role is no longer appropriate for their calling. Indeed, a neutral teacher can only miseducate the student about his coming world of turmoil, conflict, and confusion. To be of it, as citizen or leader, will require commitment and the will and courage to trust, to experiment, and to live with crises of conscience. But to have these characteristics, a child needs to be taught them, to have them cultivated—drawn out and grown. Neither exhortation nor audiovisual exposure can do this. Only one human being relating to another human being, only a human *being* these ways, can cultivate them in another.

Teachers must discard the role of the passive, neutral person who separates teaching from other roles of citizen and private person or, worse, who has no role as citizen. Instead, teachers must fuse these roles. They must be among the students' most impressive lessons in living and they must be so by doing so. If a teacher is involved in unionizing activities, or protesting Vietnam, or scuba-diving, or practicing yoga, or is fascinated with LSD or the new theologies, these should all be evident to the students.[5] The teachers' preoccupations should be a critical part of the students' educative environment. The teacher per se, as a person, should be the shape of

[5] This sentence was in the John Dewey Lecture as I gave it. When it was quoted in a press release from the University of Michigan's News Service, not unexpectedly, the reference to LSD was deleted. One can profitably speculate on why the News Service apparently thought its readers would find it acceptable for me to suggest that a teacher entertain, say, the controversial thesis that God is dead but unacceptable that the teacher explore the significance of chemically induced emotional experience. My point is that "way out" interests and activities will be a critically important part of what is creating the character of tomorrow's world—so important that children ought to have adult models to learn from who represent what it is like to be aware and involved at the cutting edge of ideas and behavior.

living in tomorrow at least as much as any representation of mooncraft or computer.

This position raises the conventional specter of "teachers brain-washing the kids." In the first place, great teachers by definition have always had a deep influence on the concerns and viewpoints of their students that goes far beyond inculcating an appreciation of the "objective" content of what is taught.

In the second place, everybody else—including the government and the advertisers—will be doing their damnedest to influence the young when they are young and when they become adults. The only way the young can learn to be aware of influences, to choose among influences, is to struggle with them. This means, in part, detecting and discriminating among the influences that *many* teachers expose them to. (A plurality of teachers, hence a plurality of influences—as in the big world—is crucial to this approach.) The world for which these youngsters have to be educated will be full of ethical dilemmas, crises of conscience, and partial and partisan definitions of "reality." Since this is also the condition of today's world, teachers who themselves behave in their role of teachers as if they personally do not have to deal with such confrontations will be miseducating the young for their confrontations tomorrow. (To be sure, there are some youth today who could and do sometimes teach their teachers these things.) To argue that the sole task of the teacher is to teach "objectivity"—how to use facts to arrive at conclusions logically, unmoved by feelings—is to assume that the facts will be a sufficient basis for decision-making. As I've indicated, this never has been the case and in new ways will not be the case in the future either.

In another way, this kind of teacher provides a necessary environment for education. Only such a teacher can be trusting and courageous enough to provide the environment in which students can practice discovering the world the teacher represents. For only such a teacher will be able to accept— indeed, to embrace—and acknowledge errors and failures in his or her actions vis-à-vis self and students as an unexceptionable part of the world. Thus, only such a teacher will be able to encourage students to discover meaningful political and social action in school and outside of it, and to explore the ramifications of the meaning of these actions for self and society. In other words, only such a teacher can provide the student access to an educative environment both unlimitedly larger than and more intimate than the conventional boundaries of the "school." And learning early to learn and grow from such an expanded educative environment is the only way to make the world of persons, institutions, and technology continually educating, continually enhancing of the cognitive and emotional capabilities described earlier. One has to learn skills in order to use symbols, in order to read a book or a computer tape, or to extract information from a library or discover what kinds of information are to be found in a library. So, too, tomorrow's involved adult must have learned the skills needed in order to learn what information his very intricate live world holds about self and society by deliberately engaging himself with individuals and circumstances in the large social system and in the many interstitial societies it will contain.

Such teachers and educational administrators seem prerequisite if we are deliberately to make a humane world in the face of the demographic and technological developments here described. But I have also argued that we cannot hope to have such an educational environment as anywhere near the norm in American education in the years immediately ahead. Thus, in the nature of the situation, what changes are to be made quickly will be made by a few teachers and administrators with the support of a few students, parents, and legislators, trustees, or other sources of moral and material support. But since we must have the products of such education as soon as possible, and since there will be relatively only a very few such products, some of us have to face up to a very upsetting question about American educational philosophy.

The question is a special case of the problem of scarcity and priorities: How do we make the most of what little we have of the organizational and motivational resources for providing effective educative experiences? Shall we continue to put our emphasis only on our traditional aim of improving education "across the board"? Or must we now acknowledge that in addition we need deliberately to try to select out and bring together the teachers and students who can best grow together for the specific purpose of providing the core of skilled leadership and skilled citizens we must have tomorrow? We don't like the traditional connotations of an "elite." But perhaps we need to invent new connotations for the term, connotations that will provide the basis for a self-fulfilling prophecy of skilled and humane leadership and citizenship.

Even if we concentrate our resources, no one can say whether enough of the needed leadership and citizenship could be created soon enough and whether they could adequately use existing institutions or implement new ones that would use their resources. Nor can anyone say whether they would know what to do or whether what they did would have the desired results. For while these accentuated intellectual and emotional skills seem to be necessary for coping with our world tomorrow, they probably aren't sufficient. The rest of the world will still be there operating in its more or less customary ways.[6] And, too, such education will not of itself eliminate the inadequacies in our knowledge and methods for doing long-range planning. All that education can do is increase the likelihood of using what we have more wisely. This may very well not be good enough.

Yet if we don't openly and seriously examine the virtue, substance, and implementation of this kind of selective education for this purpose, we will be deliberately choosing not to use our minds and feelings to discover ways of enhancing or preserving our minds and feelings. After fully and openly searching our minds, souls—and computers—it may turn out that the wise and courageous direction to take would be to hope for what we could within our present educational-political philosophy. But it might also turn out that we conclude coming circumstances require the wisdom and courage

---

[6] However, if this proposal were to be implemented, the world of the majority would have to have changed in one important respect at least. That world would have had to actively or tacitly concur in a decision to provide special education for a special portion of its population for the avowed purpose of providing a cadre of citizens better able to cope than they with the problems and opportunities of tomorrow's world. What the consequences would be for the larger portion of the society and for the "elite" of acknowledging and supporting such a need I am not prepared to explore here. (Some aspects of this sort of situation have been perceptively explored by Michael Young in his *The Rise of the Meritocracy,* Penguin Books, 1961.) Any examination of this proposal would require exploration of this issue.

to plan long-range for an especially educated cadre to help see us through the turmoil.

Whatever we decide, the decision will have to be a conscious one, and the process of decision will be painful and personal for those who struggle with it. For unless some of us are prepared to change ourselves and our institutions, unless we are prepared to risk our status and preferred perspectives in order to prepare some youth to embrace tomorrow's new opportunities and cope with its threats, we will fail. If we try to change them, to ask them to prepare themselves for a risky world, and don't make the changes in ourselves which are necessary to back them up, the sensitive among them will refuse to contribute themselves while the unperceptive will grow into fat and happy objects of manipulation. At the very least, we must share our struggle with the young. If they learn from our struggle, perhaps they may find a way out even if we don't. If they don't learn or aren't allowed to learn, I don't think there will be a way out.

INDEX

70 71 72 73   12 11 10 9 8 7 6 5 4 3 2 1

ABOUT THE AUTHOR

Donald N. Michael is Professor of Psychology and a program director, Center for Research on Utilization of Scientific Knowledge, Institute for Social Research, at The University of Michigan. He is the author of *Cybernation: The Silent Conquest, The Next Generation,* and other writings on technology and social change. He was born in 1923 and was trained as a social psychologist with a background in the physical sciences. He has worked with numerous organizations concerned with planning, cybernation, national-policy problems, and technological change. These organizations include The Joint Chiefs of Staff, the National Science Foundation, The Brookings Institution, The Peace Research Institute, and The Institute for Policy Studies. He is a Fellow of The American Association for the Advancement of Science, The American Psychological Association, and The Society for the Psychological Study of Social Issues.